Introduction

In my first cookbook *"DADGUM That's Good!"*™, we introduced you to our world of dadgum good cookin'. What's dadgum good? Well, as we've said before, it's much more than just a Southern phrase. It's our tagline for anything in our life, especially food, that's over-the-top good!

This go 'round, it's time to have more fun together as I introduce you to the heartbeat of my home — my family and friends. They are the people who have influenced my cooking and my life. I love being the chef in my own home, but I love getting everyone involved in the kitchen even more. It's been fun to eat my way through the dishes from folks I've known my whole life and those I just met on my first book tour. Truth be told, they've taught me quite a bit. I'm glad they've shared their recipes with all of you.

On each recipe, you'll be able to read through our tips/hints or some great stories from memories made through the years. After all, what's a meal without good times with good people? Just plain ol' food. In order for it to be dadgum good food, it must be shared. And once you've shared it, we hope you'll say *"DADGUM That's Good, Too!"*™

Meat and Seafood
Tips for choosing and preparing different cuts

MEAT

Here are some of the cuts of meat most commonly used.

Filet Mignon — Cut from the tenderloin, filet is a very tender cut, but lacks the beefy flavor of other cuts. Consider grilling this with a good rub or marinade.

Flank Steak — A beefy, full-flavored steak cut from the chest and side, this steak is thin and cooks quickly. To retain the juices in the meat, let it rest for a few minutes before carving against the grain.

Porterhouse and T-Bone — Cut extra thick, these give you the taste and texture of the strip and the tenderloin. To prevent them from overcooking, sear the steaks with the strip portion facing the hottest part of the fire and the tenderloin facing the cooler side.

Rib-Eye Steak — Cut from the rib, they are very tender, beefy and well-marbled with fat, which makes them great for grilling and smoking. They should be thick and seared over a medium-high heat. Move to a cooler spot on the grill to finish.

Sirloin, New York Strip and Prime Rib — Full-flavored premium cuts that have a natural flavor, which you may want to bring out with a little salt, pepper, and olive oil.

Brisket — The brisket consists of two different muscles. The top muscle, known as the "point," is fibrous and difficult to cut. The flat is leaner and more even, which makes it easier to cut. It's likely that you'll find the second cut in your local supermarket, trimmed with a thin layer of fat on the top. If it's untrimmed, trim the fat down to 1/4-inch thickness. To test your brisket for tenderness, hold the middle of the brisket in your hand. If the ends give, you've picked the right one. A rigid brisket is a sign that you're in for a tough time.

Spare Ribs — Pick ribs that are between 2 and 4 pounds. Smaller ribs are likely to come from a younger animal and will cook faster because they're more tender.

St. Louis Style Ribs — These specially trimmed ribs are lighter than spare ribs, topping out at about 2 pounds.

Baby Back Ribs — These flavorsome ribs are great if you're smoking for the first time. Baby Backs are a little more expensive, but they're the most tender and cook faster than spare ribs.

Pork Butts and Picnics — Similar cuts with different bones. There is not much difference between them, but they do offer a choice. You can remove the bone or cook them bone-in.

▶ tip

Meat cooked on the bone shrinks less. It also allows you to quickly test for tenderness. When the meat is ready, the bone slides out easily. Buy your butt with the fat on and trim it to suit your taste. And remember — fat equals flavor.

FISH

Mahi-Mahi — Similar in texture to swordfish, but it's a little oilier. Despite this, it dries out quickly on the grill, so you might want to brine it.

Red Snapper — Quick and easy to grill or fry. If you grill, handle carefully. Make sure the fish and the grill are well-oiled.

Salmon — A favorite for grilling because it doesn't dry out. It's rich in healthy, natural oils and fats, so you can pop it on the grill without oiling. Its flavor also complements stronger marinades.

Scallops — You'll want to use fresh ocean scallops if you're grilling or frying them. Take a close look at the scallops before you buy them. If they're unnaturally white and are sitting in a milky liquid, they're processed. Natural scallops are a pinkish tan or ivory. They have a firmer texture and a bigger surface area that holds the batter better.

Trout — Freshwater trout is great on the grill. The skin becomes thin and crispy and the flesh is flavorful without an overpowering fishiness.

Tuna — Does best using a simple marinade of herbs and oil. This prevents it from drying out and getting tough. If you like your tuna rare, buy 1 1/2-inch thick steaks. This will enable you to sear them without overcooking them.

▶ tip

Fish smokes fast, so it requires a little more attention. The best types of fish to test in your smoker are salmon and trout fillets. Boneless fish fillets are the easiest to smoke. Fish with a higher fat content, such as trout, salmon, tuna and mackerel, retain their moisture better during smoking. Most fish should be brined and air-dried before smoking.

SEAFOOD

Mussels — Versatile, quick and cheap. They steam beautifully and within minutes you can rustle up a satisfying gourmet dish.

Shrimp — Taste great any way you cook them. Though some prefer boiled shrimp, there's a lot to be said for steaming them. It retains the delicate flavor better.

USDA* Safe Minimum Internal Temperatures

Beef, Pork, Veal, Lamb (Ground)	160°F
Beef, Pork, Veal and Lamb Steaks, Roasts and Chops	145°F
Egg Dishes	160°F
Fish	145°F
Turkey, Chicken and Duck Whole, Pieces and Ground	165°F

* United States Department of Agriculture

Smoking Times and Temperatures

Beef

Item	Size	Temp	Time	Internal Temp
Beef Ribs	Full Rack	225°F	4–5 hours	175°F
Brisket	6–12 pounds	250°F	1 hour per pound	180°F–190°F
Roast (Chuck, rump, sirloin tip)	4–5 pounds	225°F	3–4 hours	125°F Rare 145°F Medium 165°F Well done

Game

Item	Size	Temp	Time	Internal Temp
Cornish Game Hens 2 whole	1.5 pounds each	225°F	4 hours	165°F
Dove, Pheasant, Quail	12–16 birds	200°F	2–3 hours	180–185°F Well done
Duck	4–6 pounds	250°F	2.5–4 hours	165°F

Pork

Item	Size	Temp	Time	Internal Temp
Baby Back Ribs (Unwrapped)	2 slabs	225°F	4–5 hours	165°F
Baby Back Ribs (Wrapped)	2 slabs	225°F	5–6 hours wrapped during last 1.5 to 2 hours	165°F
Loin Rib End Roast	4–6 pounds	200°F	4.5–7 hours	170°F Well done (Meat should pull away from bone)
Loin Roast (Boneless)	3–4 pounds	250°F	2 hours	165°F Well done (Meat should pull away from bone)
Pork Butt (Sliced)	4–5 pounds	225°F	1 hour to 1.25 hours per pound	165°F
Pork Butt (Pulled)	4–5 pounds	250°F	2.5 hours unwrapped + 2.5 hours wrapped	195°F
Short Ribs	4–5 pounds	200°F	2.5–3.5 hours	165°F

Poultry

Item	Size	Temp	Time	Internal Temp
Chicken Breasts (Bone-in)	3 count	225°F	1–1.5 hours per pound	165°F
Chicken Breasts (Boneless)	3 count	225°F	45 min. per pound	165°F
Chicken Quarters	4 count	225°F	3–3.5 hours	165°F
Chicken Thighs	12 count	225°F	2 hours	165°F
Whole Chicken	3–5 pounds	225°F–250°F	45 min. to 1 hour per pound	165°F
Whole Turkey	8–12 pounds	225°F	30–35 min. per pound	165°F

Seafood

Item	Size	Temp	Time	Internal Temp
Fish	2 pounds of fillets	225°F	35–45 minutes	145°F Flakes with a fork
Salmon	2–3 pounds	200°F	2.5–3.5 hours	145°F Flakes with a fork
Shrimp	Full Grate	225°F	1–2 hours Based on size of shrimp	145°F Will be pink/shells open

Vegetables

Item	Size	Temp	Time	Internal Temp
Asparagus	1.5 pounds	250°F	1.5 hours	Until tender
Cabbage	Whole	250°F	3–4 hours	Until tender
Green Beans	2 -14.25 oz. cans	250°F	2 hours	Until tender
Lima Beans	1 2-pound package	225°F	8 hours	Until tender
Sweet Potatoes	8 large	275°F	1 hour unwrapped + 1 hour wrapped	Until tender

Direct versus Indirect Grilling

DIRECT — Direct grilling is a fast method; the heat is high and the cooking time is shorter. With direct grilling, the food is placed directly above the heat source (charcoal, propane or electric). This type of grilling method works best for vegetables, hamburgers or steaks. It's important to stand by your grill when using direct heat and watch the food carefully so it won't burn. Make sure you turn the food as necessary. Close the lid of your grill to get a good sear, but again, don't leave that grill unattended.

INDIRECT — The indirect method of grilling involves placing your food on the grill away from the direct heat source. This means you need to keep your coals or flame off to the side of the food, not directly under it. This is a slower method of grilling, which will require a longer cooking time, but it is much more forgiving. Indirect grilling works great for pork roast, ribs, whole chicken, turkey and beef brisket.

Most Common Woods for Smoking

When you are testing out a new wood flavor, make sure you begin with a small amount. See how you like the flavor, then increase the amount you use when smoking.

Alder wood gives off a light flavor that works well with fish and poultry. It makes a perfect pairing with salmon.

Apple gives a very sweet, mild flavor to your food. It pairs well with poultry and pork. Apple wood will turn chicken skin dark brown. With this wood, it does take a longer cooking time to infuse the smoke flavor. Be careful not to oversmoke your food, which will result in a bitter taste.

Cherry has a mild, sweet flavor and pairs well with most foods. This wood is great for poultry and fish.

Hickory will add a strong smoke flavor; be careful not to overuse. This wood pairs best with pork, beef and lamb. It is available in most areas.

Mesquite is great for smoking and can also be used when grilling. It burns hot and fast, so be prepared to use more wood. Mesquite is a great alternative to hickory and has a milder flavor. It pairs well with most any meat and is especially good for brisket and hamburgers.

Oak wood gives a strong smoke flavor, without easily overpowering your food. It pairs well with beef or lamb.

Pecan burns cooler than other woods and provides a mild flavor. It pairs well with pork and is a great substitute for hickory.

These woods are also used for smoking, but are less common: Almond, Apricot, Ash, Birch, Black Walnut, Citrus (lemon, orange), Crabapple, Grapefruit, Lilac, Maple, Mulberry, Peach, Pear, Plum, Walnut.

Avoid these woods, as they contain sap and will not give off a complementary taste or smell: Cedar, Cypress, Elm, Eucalyptus, Fir, Pine, Redwood, Sassafras, Spruce, Sycamore.

CHIPS, CHUNKS, LOGS OR PELLETS?

The cut of wood you choose depends on the type of equipment you use for smoking. For most large barrel-type smokers or charcoal smokers, you'll want to use chunks. Wood chips are most commonly used for propane and electric smokers. Some grills are equipped with an accessory smoker box for adding wood. Pellets are reserved for specialty-type grills or smokers. There is a difference between the type of pellets that are used for a heat source versus the pellets that are used for cooking, so make sure you purchase the correct type. Championship BBQ competitors use very large smokers designed for larger wood logs or chunks. Whether you are smoking on a small electric smoker on your back porch or a trailer-sized smokehouse, we're sure you can create a dadgum good result with the smoked recipes in this book!

Dadgum Good Flavors and Such

"DADGUM THAT'S GOOD!"™ DRY RUB

Makes about 3/4 cup

Instructions

1. In an airtight container or bowl, combine salt, sugar, paprika, garlic powder, celery seeds, black pepper and cayenne pepper. Use as a rub on chicken, pork or beef, or just sprinkle on meat when grilling. Also, use as a seasoning for vegetables on the grill or in the smoker or steamer.

You'll Need

- 4 tablespoons salt
- 2 tablespoons granulated sugar
- 2 tablespoons paprika
- 2 tablespoons garlic powder
- 2 tablespoons ground celery seeds
- 1 tablespoon freshly ground black pepper
- 1 teaspoon cayenne pepper

"DADGUM THAT'S GOOD!"™ SEASONING

Makes 1/2 cup

Instructions

1. In a medium bowl, combine dark and light brown sugars, paprika, lemon pepper, onion salt, garlic powder, celery salt, ginger, basil, sage, peppercorns and marjoram. Use as a seasoning on chicken, pork or beef, or just sprinkle on meat when grilling. Also, use as a seasoning for vegetables on the grill or in the smoker or steamer.

You'll Need

- 2 1/2 tablespoons dark brown sugar
- 1 1/2 teaspoons light brown sugar
- 1 tablespoon paprika
- 1 teaspoon lemon pepper
- 3/4 teaspoon onion salt
- 1/2 teaspoon garlic powder
- 1/2 teaspoon celery salt
- 1/2 teaspoon ground ginger
- 1/2 teaspoon dried basil
- 1/2 teaspoon crushed sage
- 1/2 teaspoon cracked black peppercorns
- 1/4 teaspoon ground marjoram

"DADGUM THAT'S GOOD!"™ BBQ SAUCE

Makes 2 cups

Instructions

1. In a medium saucepan over medium heat, combine olive oil and garlic and cook, stirring frequently, until golden, about 20 minutes. Remove from heat and let garlic cool in the oil.

2. Whisk in ketchup, honey, vinegar, soy sauce and espresso. Return to heat and simmer for 15 minutes to blend flavors. Remove from heat. Serve sauce heated.

You'll Need

- 2 tablespoons extra virgin olive oil
- 2 tablespoons minced garlic
- 1 cup ketchup
- 1 cup honey
- 1/2 cup balsamic vinegar
- 1/4 cup soy sauce
- 1/4 cup Starbucks® double shot espresso or strong home-brewed coffee

---

"DADGUM THAT'S GOOD!"™ BRINE

Makes enough to brine 1 whole chicken or turkey

Instructions

1. In a large stockpot, heat 2 cups water with salt, brown sugar, peppercorns, garlic, basil, rosemary, onion powder, ginger, soy sauce and Worcestershire sauce. Bring to a boil, stirring well. Let cool.

2. When cooled, add 2 gallons ice water, stirring well. Place turkey, chicken or other meat in a container and pour brining mixture over. Cover and brine in the refrigerator for at least 8 or up to 12 hours. When you remove your meat, rinse it well, inside and out, if necessary, to avoid being too salty after cooking. This is a very important step. After thoroughly rinsing all salt off, pat dry, and cook according to your recipe.

You'll Need

- 2 cups water
- 2 cups kosher salt
- 2 cups packed brown sugar
- 1/4 cup cracked black peppercorns
- 3 tablespoons chopped garlic cloves
- 2 tablespoons chopped fresh basil leaves
- 2 tablespoons chopped fresh rosemary
- 2 tablespoons onion powder
- 1 tablespoon ground ginger
- 1/2 cup soy sauce
- 1/2 cup Worcestershire sauce
- 2 gallons ice water

Top Left: *John Darin McLemore at 2 years old.*
Top Right: *Family photo: 1969.*
Middle: *I still love to talk on the phone.*
Bottom: *Ornamental iron was the beginning.*

Top: *Our family was the sales department in the early days.*
Middle: *Working in the shop got us real dirty.*

Our Story...

For as long as I can remember, I've always loved to cook. I suppose you could say this was an inherited trait. When your father invented and manufactured cooking products, with his little ones right by his side, it was hard not to fall in love with the idea of cooking for large crowds. Being a cooking products manufacturer wasn't always in the cards for my family. It all started with my dad — Dawson. He was a master "tinkerer" who honed his skills in the backyard with a welder, determination and lots (and I do mean LOTS) of steel.

We moved to Columbus, Georgia, in 1971, and Dad began focusing more on that tinkering in the backyard and taught us all how to weld. In fact, the running joke was that I had a diaper in one hand and a welder in the other! Wherever my dad was, I wanted to be. Whatever my dad did, I wanted to do. He was and still is my absolute hero. His tinkering started to take on a life much bigger than a backyard could handle and, well, the rest is history. History that led to the birth of Masterbuilt. There's no way I can share my story without sharing some of the Masterbuilt story because it's been such a huge part of my life. In my first cookbook, I shared the history of our company. This go-round, I'd like for you to hear it from the man responsible for me and Masterbuilt — Dawson McLemore. If you ever meet us, you'll hear me call him Ole' Man, and I explain why on the recipe for Ole' Man's Steak (page 161). Now, let's hear what the Ole' Man remembers....

Masterbuilt Story

Here's the Masterbuilt story, as told by my dad, Dawson McLemore.

Dawson McLemore

In 1972, I was a salesman for Goodyear Tire. As a hobby, I loved spending time in our backyard with my sons, welding and making something useful from metal. One of the first things we made were brackets for hanging plant baskets. My wife needed something to hold her plants, so I made her some brackets. With a family of seven, I was always open to any opportunity to add to our income, so I took some of these brackets to the nursery to sell. I also noticed some fern stands at the nursery and making one for my wife turned into selling more than you could shake a stick at. John was about 8 years old and would load those fern stands up in his little red wagon and take them door-to-door. He was my first traveling salesman! Eventually, we started making baker's racks and officially started our company — M&M Welding. While I was driving to Alabama one day, I was having a conversation with the good Lord about our business. You see, I had quit my job at Goodyear and lost all of my benefits. I had a wife and five children to support at home and felt like I needed help running the business. I said in that prayer, "Lord, if you'll help me, I'll make you a business partner and rename this business after you." The name Masterbuilt came to me right then. Ever since that day, the "Master" has been leading Masterbuilt.

Most of you probably know Masterbuilt for cooking products, not baker's racks and fern stands. How that came about all started with a Snapper lawnmower. I made a fish cooker and bartered it for the lawnmower. I thought, if it was good enough to barter, it was good enough to sell. And that's how we got into the fish cooker business.

When John and the rest of my boys were little, they could have spent more time playing sports or focusing on schoolwork, but they seemed to always love helping me with Masterbuilt.

Top Left: Goodyear corporate photo of Dawson.
Top Right: Future ballplayer? or not!
Below: Yes! I was a high school graduate. Class of 1983.

- the following text appears within the news clipping images:

Fire destroys plant near downtown Columbus

A Columbus firefighter is silhouetted by sparks as he saws through a chain-link fence to get better access to the fire at Masterbuilt Manufacturing Inc. at 1645 Second Ave.

Columbus fire officials were unsure what started a blaze which caused explosive noises and destroyed the Masterbuilt Manufacturing Inc. plant on Second Avenue early Friday.

"We have no idea how it started," said Chief Robert Spence of Welding supplies used in manufacturing did not explode, nor did they "pose a serious problem in fighting the fire,"

The blaze apparently started near the middle of the building, where cardboard and shipping materials were stored, he said.

Masterbuilt makes gas grills, propane tanks and fish cookers.

Firefighters received the call about

Rising from the ashes

Top Left: News articles from Masterbuilt fire, 1991.

Top Right: Me with the Ole' Man and Momma.

Above: Me and my brother Don with the Ole' Man.

John stayed in high school and got his diploma, but he'll be quick to tell you that was for his Momma. When the rest of his friends were hanging out in Panama City Beach, Florida, after graduation, John showed up for work on Monday. He opted for the University of Masterbuilt instead of college. He didn't even let a serious accident with a grinder back when he was 13 years old discourage him. And let me tell you, that was a scary day. I remember throwing him in the back of my truck and letting my 15-year-old son Don drive us to the hospital. Don didn't even have a license! The surgeon put John's arm back together and he went back to work. Years later, when we had a serious fire at Masterbuilt and most of our equipment was burned up, I had a decision to make. We would either shut down or bring it back. I knew that Masterbuilt had a lot of life left in it for my family, so we started building cookers with the equipment we had left.

I still remember John bringing me the first fish cooker they made after the fire and placing it on my desk. John said, "Ole' Man, here's cooker number one and we're back in business."

There's a certain time in a man's life when he knows he needs to move on. That time for me was age 47, when I retired from Masterbuilt and left it in my boys' hands. John had a vision to take the company to the next level and he's never stopped. I'm tickled to see how far Masterbuilt has come. It isn't just a company; it's a part of our family. I wouldn't have handed over the reins to anyone else and I have to tell you, John sure has made this Ole' Man proud.

A Love Story

Masterbuilt may have been my first love, but Tonya McLemore is my one true love. From the moment we met, I knew my life was forever changed. My story isn't my story without Tonya. As for our story, let's hear about that from her...

Tonya McLemore

When I was in college, my parent's rented a townhouse in Panama City Beach, Florida, from Dawson and Evelyn McLemore, for our family vacation. The McLemores made a stop by the townhouse on their way down to the Florida Keys to pick up scuba diving gear. Dawson and Evelyn instantly connected with my parents, Wes and Shirley. The McLemores told me about their son John. Truth be told, I knew who John was. We graduated from rival high schools on the same year and, let's just say, he dated a lot of girls! My mom and John's mom started putting their heads together from that moment. You see, Mrs. McLemore had just had a conversation with John where he declared his intentions to "settle down" with a good girl. She was pretty sure she had just met that good girl. The McLemores went on down to the Keys and met up with their sons, John and Don. Unbeknownst to me, I was a topic of conversation on their boat. John's mom told him they met a girl he might need to ask out and that I had a "great personality." From those two words, John became instantly uninterested. I later found out that his dad pulled him to the side and said, "Son, you need to call that girl." John knew that meant great personality and cute, so he called me when they got back from the Keys! He asked me over to his house for dinner and cooked steak and the lobster that he brought back from Florida.

We dated for three months and, quite honestly, I got scared. John fell head-over-heels in love with me and was ready to settle down. I was still in college and just not ready for that serious commitment. I broke things off and went off to Auburn University to finish up college. In the meantime, our parents were still conspiring to get us back together. I had my sights set on meeting some clean-cut college guy at Auburn and had left John behind, working in the shop at Masterbuilt. John was so heartbroken that he poured himself into his work. He lived at Masterbuilt during that time, literally sleeping in the shop. I later found out he even invented a new product during that time! Although he became obsessed with work, his heartbreak also left him distracted. His dad will tell you that after several small

Top Left: The trip that started it all. Lobstering with Momma, Dad and Don.

Above: Our engagement picture. Can you see the rock on her hand?

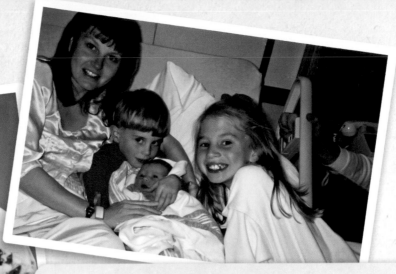

accidents in the shop, he turned to John one day, pointed his finger at him and said, "GO HOME, sport! And don't come back until you get your head on straight!"

Soon after, I heard that John was going to be baptized at a local church and I was so proud for him, so I attended and sat in the back of the church with my mom. I didn't say anything to him and slipped out quietly afterward. I realized that not only was I proud for him, I also missed him.

John knew I attended the baptism and called me afterward to thank me. His territory for Masterbuilt included the Auburn, Alabama area, so I told him to drop by my apartment some time to visit. He did, and we've been together ever since.

We met in July of 1986 and we got engaged in July of 1987, on our one-year anniversary. We were married in August of 1988, the day before my birthday. I began my student teaching that fall and graduated in December with a teaching degree. We had our daughter Brooke on May 28, 1990 and our son, J-Mac, on July 29, 1992. Our daughter Bailey was born on Valentine's Day in 1998 — our very own love child! Every day with John is an adventure and that day was no exception. I had a planned delivery and on the way to the hospital he decided to speed through a 45 MPH zone. We were pulled over by a policeman, so I had to fake labor to get us out of a ticket! We rode the rest of the way with a police escort. Like I said — always an adventure!

Life's funny sometimes and it gives you some full circle moments. Brooke is in college now to become a teacher, just like her mom. Our son, J-Mac, is following in his father's footsteps at Masterbuilt. Bailey loves to cook, just like her dad, and plans to also be a teacher.

From our very first blind date when John cooked for me, so much of our life has centered around cooking together and spending time around the table. These cookbooks are more than pages filled with recipes; they are scrapbooks of our family memories. John's the love of my life and the rock of our family. With him by my side, life is pretty dadgum good!

Top Left: *Our wedding day.*
Top Right: *Our family is complete.*
Above: *Our family today.*

Dadgum Good Times

My favorite times are the ones spent with family and friends. For us McLemores, much of that gathering time is spent around the table, sharing dadgum good meals. Is there anything better than downtime with the people you love, filling your belly and your heart?! As you make your way through the recipes in this book, my hope is that you enjoy more than just good food, but also dadgum good stories and memories with my family and friends.

Our times on the road representing our Masterbuilt products, and on the *"DADGUM That's Good!"*™ book tour, have been nothing short of exciting. From trade shows in the 1980s to television shows now, we've been feeding people all over the country. I'm often asked, "Are you a chef?" And my reply is always the same — I'm a cook. Much like the way I had a passion for business from a young age and learned by trial and error, I learned to cook the same way. And you know what? So can you. In a day and age in which being a "foodie" is very trendy, don't ever be intimidated in the kitchen or at your backyard BBQ. Just go for it and make each recipe your own.

Top: Wherever we are....
Left: We eat some dadgum good food!
Right: "DADGUM That's Good!"™ book tour.

Top Left: Nice looking young couple.

Top Right: Momma was prettier than Mary Kay.

Middle: What a great love story.

Bottom: Our last Christmas with my momma.

Growing up, our home was the place to be. All of my friends wanted to hang out at my house and my parents were constantly cooking and entertaining crowds. Through 50 years of marriage, their love story was such an inspiration. Although it may have been a bit awkward at the time, I've learned to appreciate that my friends thought my mom was the "hot" mom! Dawson and Evelyn were a pretty neat couple and they were always having fun. There's a strong sense of security that comes from having parents that love each other so much and share family meals around the table.

It's many years later and now my home is THE place to be. On any given day, you can find all sorts of kids — from teenagers to college students — hanging out around our house. They eat up all of our food, sleep all over our sofas and floor, and make tons of noise — and we wouldn't have it any other way! I've heard that the perfect job is one you love so much you'd do it for free, but you're so good at it you get paid. I'd say I have the perfect job. I get to manufacture cooking products for families like mine — and yours — to enjoy time with one another around the table. Even better — I've been able to write these cookbooks and share the food, and the love, with all of you.

— John McLemore

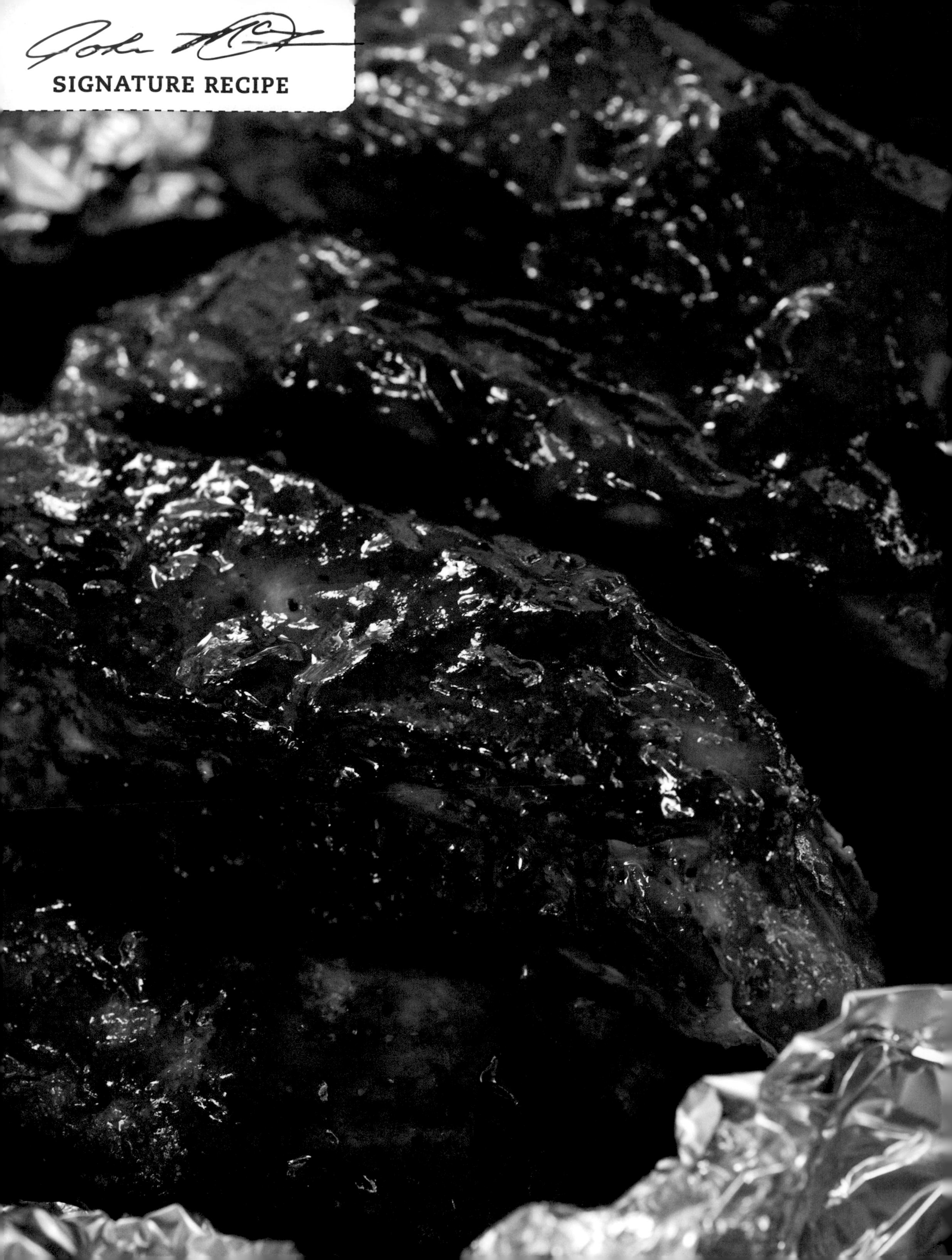

SIGNATURE RECIPE

REDNECK RIBS
Serves 6

Where I'm from, being called a "redneck" is a compliment. I drive a 4x4 truck, love to mud ride, and wear dirty boots with blue jeans to business meetings. Ribs are a favorite menu item of most rednecks and we don't need a plate when we eat them. We just stand around the smoker and eat while we swap stories. My wife doesn't mind that I'm a redneck, as long as I'm a redneck who treats her right! You don't have to be from the South to be a redneck, or to enjoy these dadgum good redneck ribs.

Instructions

1. Preheat smoker to 225°F.

2. **BBQ Sauce:** Meanwhile, in a small saucepan over medium heat, combine ketchup, apple jelly, steak sauce and brown sugar and heat until well blended. Set aside.

3. In a medium bowl, combine salt, pepper, onion powder and garlic powder. Rub mixture on the ribs. Place ribs on middle rack in smoker and smoke for 1 hour. Remove ribs and baste with BBQ sauce. Double-wrap in heavy-duty aluminum foil and return to smoker. Smoke for another 2 hours or until internal temperature reaches 165°F. Then remove and baste with more sauce and serve!

You'll Need

BBQ Sauce

*   1 cup ketchup
*   3/4 cup apple jelly
*   1/2 cup steak sauce
*   1/4 cup packed brown sugar

*   1 teaspoon salt
*   1 teaspoon freshly ground black pepper
*   1/2 teaspoon onion powder
*   1/2 teaspoon garlic powder
*   4 pounds country-style pork ribs (sliced with bone-in)

❱ suggested wood
HICKORY

Me and my friend Gary eating our redneck ribs in Memphis!

SMOKED SHRIMP AND GRITS

Serves 8

Shrimp and Grits is one of those dishes that is certainly regional. Folks in New Orleans, Charleston, Nashville, Gulf Shores, and so on all have their favorite versions of this recipe. We think the best Shrimp and Grits recipe is the one you make at home and enjoy with your family and friends. Start with our recipe, but don't be afraid to change it up and add your own ingredients. One piece of advice is to make sure you don't oversmoke this recipe. Drain the butter off of the smoked shrimp before adding to the grits because butter strongly absorbs the smoke. You want a hint of smoke flavor, but you don't want this dish to be overpowered with smoke.

Instructions

1. Preheat smoker to 225°F.

2. Cook grits according to package directions. Stir cream cheese, Velveeta, egg, minced garlic, Worcestershire sauce, mustard, pepper and salt to taste into cooked grits, while still hot. Place grits in a deep-dish round disposable aluminum foil pan, cover tightly with heavy-duty aluminum foil, place in smoker and smoke for 30 to 45 minutes or until cheese is melted. Remove, stir well and set side.

3. **Shrimp:** Meanwhile, in a small disposable aluminum foil pan, place melted butter, shrimp, Cajun seasoning, red and green peppers and onion. Stir well. Place shrimp mixture in preheated smoker on middle rack and smoke for 30 minutes. Remove and completely drain off any excess butter. (This step of draining off the butter is key, as it will keep the dish from being overwhelmed by smoke flavor.) Top each serving of grits with shrimp mixture and sprinkle with smoked paprika.

You'll Need

- 1 cup uncooked grits
- 6 ounces cream cheese, cubed
- 4 ounces Velveeta cheese, cubed
- 1 egg, well beaten
- 3 cloves garlic, minced
- 1 tablespoon Worcestershire sauce
- 1 teaspoon Dijon mustard
- 1/4 teaspoon freshly ground black pepper
- Salt
- Pinch smoked paprika

Shrimp

- 1/2 cup butter, melted
- 1 1/2 pounds medium shrimp, peeled, deveined and thoroughly washed
- 1/2 teaspoon Cajun seasoning
- 1 red bell pepper, thinly sliced
- 1/2 green bell pepper, thinly sliced
- 1 medium white onion, thinly sliced

❯ suggested wood
HICKORY

CORN CHOWDER
Serves 6 to 8

This recipe calls for using prepackaged ham chunks and infusing them with smokey flavor. The prepackaged ham is good if you are short on time, but I recommend using our Sweet 'n' Spicy Smoked Ham on page 70 or our Aloha Ham on page 79. This will take the chowder from good to dadgum good!

Instructions

1. Preheat smoker to 225°F.

2. Place 1 1/2 cups ham chunks and 1/2 cup of water in an 8-inch square disposable aluminum foil pan. Place on middle rack of smoker and smoke for about 50 minutes.

3. Meanwhile, in a Dutch oven over medium heat, cook bacon slices. Drain bacon, reserving drippings, and crumble bacon. Set aside. Add celery and onion to reserved drippings and cook, stirring frequently, for 25 to 30 minutes or until tender. Cut corn from cobs and add to vegetables. Add remaining 1 cup of water. Simmer on a gentle boil for 10 minutes. Remove ham from smoker and add 1 1/2 cups of the ham chunks, milk and 1/2 cup of the half-and-half cream to Dutch oven. Keep on low, so milk will not scorch. Add parsley, sugar, basil, salt and pepper.

4. In a saucepan over medium heat, combine flour, remaining 1/2 cup of half-and-half cream and 1/4 cup of the hot chowder liquid, stirring well. Add to chowder, while stirring constantly, until well mixed. Cook for 15 to 20 minutes, until mixture is thickened. Sprinkle with crumbled bacon and serve. (Excess ham can be frozen for later use.)

You'll Need

- 1 (16-ounce) prepackaged ham chunks
- 1 1/2 cups water, divided
- 10 slices thick bacon
- 3/4 cup finely sliced celery
- 1 medium yellow onion, chopped
- 8 ears corn
- 1 cup milk
- 1 cup half-and-half cream, divided
- 3 teaspoons finely chopped fresh parsley
- 1 teaspoon granulated sugar
- 1/2 teaspoon dried basil
- 1/2 teaspoon salt
- 1/2 teaspoon freshly ground black pepper
- 2 tablespoons self-rising flour

❯ suggested wood
MESQUITE

SMOKED SAUSAGE
Serves 4 to 5

Who doesn't love food from the State Fair?! While this recipe is great when served over rice at the dinner table, another tasty option is to serve up the sausage, peppers and onions on a soft hoagie bun. You'll swear you stood in line at the fairgrounds for this warm, delicious sandwich. And when you eat this at home, you won't have to worry about getting on a roller coaster with a full stomach!

Instructions

1. Cook rice according to package directions.

2. Meanwhile, preheat smoker to 250°F.

3. Place hot and mild sausage on middle rack of smoker and smoke for 1 1/4 hours, turning once halfway through cooking.

4. In a skillet, heat oil over medium heat. Add red and green peppers, onion and seasoning and cook, stirring frequently, until crisp-tender, 25 to 30 minutes.

5. Remove sausage from smoker and slice into 1/2-inch slices. Serve over rice, topped with pepper and onion mixture.

You'll Need

- 1 1/2 cups long-grain and wild rice, garlic and olive oil-flavored, such as Uncle Ben's or your favorite type

- 1 pound hot Italian sausage in casing

- 1 pound mild Italian sausage in casing

- 2 tablespoons olive oil

- 1 large red bell pepper, cut into 1/4-inch strips

- 1 large green bell pepper, cut into 1/4-inch strips

- 1 large sweet onion, cut into 1/4-inch slices

- 1 1/4 teaspoons "DADGUM That's Good!"™ Seasoning (page 12)

▶ suggested wood
MESQUITE

You'll Need

- 1 whole cabbage
- 3 chicken or beef bouillon cubes
- 1/2 cup butter or margarine
- 1 tablespoon steak seasoning or rub
- 1/4 teaspoon salt

SMOKED CABBAGE
Serves 4

My brother Don and I were in South Dakota filming a cooking segment for a sportsman's show. We drove to the location where the movie "Dances with Wolves" was filmed. I remember looking in all directions and I could see no evidence of civilization. It was quite a peaceful place to work and we filmed 13 recipes in one day! This smoked cabbage was one of those recipes. It was perfect for an on-location shoot, since there is no need for a dish; only heavy-duty foil. Whether you're at home or in the middle of nowhere, you'll enjoy this simple recipe.

Instructions

1. Preheat smoker to 250°F.

2. Remove core from cabbage. Place bouillon cubes and butter in center of cabbage. Season cabbage with steak seasoning and salt.

3. Wrap cabbage in foil, leaving an opening at the top. Smoke for 3 to 4 hours until tender.

▶ suggested wood
HICKORY

BRINED RED SNAPPER STEAKS
Serves 6

My dad was in the military and traveled overseas. During his travels he learned the Japanese word "Ichiban." He later named his fishing boat "Ichiban" and my momma would always ask him what it meant. He wouldn't tell her, but promised to let her know on their 25th wedding anniversary. It was a running conversation-starter through the years when we would go fishing and people would ask about the name. We caught a lot of red snapper and made tons of family memories on that boat. On my parent's 25th anniversary, momma found out what she probably could have guessed all along — "Ichiban" means "number one."

Instructions

1. Fill water pan and add liquid shrimp boil. Preheat smoker to 225°F.

2. In a medium saucepan over medium-high heat, combine water and salt. Bring to a boil, reduce heat to low and simmer until salt is dissolved. Add honey, lemon slices and ginger and simmer for 1 minute. Let mixture cool slightly. Add ice water.

3. Place steaks in a pan or plastic gallon resealable freezer bag and pour brine over. Cover and refrigerate and brine for at least 4 hours, turning halfway through brining time, unless the steaks are completely covered by the liquid. Remove after 4 hours and place, skin side down, on lightly greased middle rack of smoker and smoke for 40 minutes or until internal temperature reaches 145°F. Sprinkle each steak lightly with Cajun seasoning and parsley flakes immediately after they finish cooking.

Brine Optional
We recommend using our "DADGUM That's Good!"™ Brine (page 13) as another option to the brining ingredients listed in Step 2.

You'll Need
- 1 tablespoon liquid shrimp boil
- 1 cup water
- 1 tablespoon kosher salt
- 1/2 cup honey
- 1 lemon, sliced
- 1/2 tablespoon ground ginger
- 1 cup ice water
- 2 pounds red snapper, cut into 6 steaks (each 3/4- to 1-inch thick)
- Cajun seasoning
- Dried parsley flakes

▶ suggested wood
HICKORY

Dawson in the Navy.

TOM'S EUROPEAN FILET APPETIZER
Serves 6 to 8

We have traveled all over the world to participate in trade shows. We sometimes hire food stylists or chefs to work the booths with us and prep food. When we were in Cologne, Germany, at the International Hardware Fair, Chef Tom helped out in our booth and he gave us this phenomenal recipe. It's definitely not a dish this Southern boy would have come up with (see: Redneck Ribs!), but as far as I'm concerned, dadgum good food from anywhere deserves a spot in my book.

Instructions

1.   Preheat smoker to 225°F.

2.   Season filets generously with steak seasoning. Place on middle rack of smoker and smoke at 225°F for 3 hours for medium or until internal temperature reaches 145°F (see Doneness Chart to the right).

3.   Let meat rest until room temperature and then refrigerate to cool for 1 to 4 hours.

4.   Slice filet as thin as possible and place slices on plate, covering entire plate. Add a stack of arugula in center of plate. Sprinkle tomatoes and shaved Parmesan over arugula and meat. Garnish with pine nuts, if using, and freshly ground black pepper.

5.   Drizzle with lemon juice, olive oil and balsamic vinegar.

You'll Need

- 3 beef loin filets or wild game (each about 1 1/2 pounds)
- Steak seasoning
- Arugula or baby spinach leaves
- 1/2 cup cherry tomatoes, halved
- 1/4 cup shaved Parmesan cheese
- Pine nuts (optional)
- Freshly ground black pepper
- 1 tablespoon fresh lemon juice
- 1 tablespoon olive oil
- 1 teaspoon balsamic vinegar

Doneness Chart

125°F Rare

135°F Medium-Rare

145°F Medium

155°F Medium-Well

165°F Well Done

❱ suggested wood
HICKORY

SMOKEY STUFFED BURGERS
Serves 6 to 8

Grilled burgers are a favorite in backyards all around the world. Smoking burgers is a fun and delicious way to change up your burger routine. The smoking process gives a juicy result and adds tons of flavor to these stuffed burgers. You can use this same recipe on the grill. In fact, why not try both and have your guests do a taste-off to see which one they prefer. My vote is both!

Instructions

1. Preheat smoker to 275°F.

2. In a large bowl, combine ground chuck, ground round, Heinz 57 Sauce and A1 Steak Sauce.

3. In a medium saucepan, heat oil over medium-high heat. Add mushrooms and onion and cook until softened, about 25 minutes. Sprinkle lightly with garlic salt. Cut cheese into 16 squares.

4. Using a 1/3-cup measure, shape beef mixture to make 16 patties. (They don't have to be perfect!) On eight of the patties, place one square of cheese, then 1 1/2 tablespoons of the mushroom mixture and top with another square of cheese. Place another plain patty on top and pinch edges to seal. Reshape the edges with your fingers to round out. Sprinkle lightly with pepper.

5. Place burgers on third rack of smoker and smoke for 1 hour or until internal temperature reaches 145°F and meat is no longer pink inside.

You'll Need

- 2 pounds ground chuck
- 1 pound ground round
- 1/2 cup Heinz 57 Sauce
- 1/2 cup A1 Steak Sauce
- 4 tablespoons extra virgin olive oil
- 1 cup chopped sliced mushrooms
- 1/2 finely chopped large yellow onion
- Garlic salt
- 4 slices extra-thick Velveeta cheese slices
- Freshly ground black pepper

❯ suggested wood
HICKORY

One of the most popular dishes from our first cookbook was Four-Cheese Smoked Mac n' Cheese. Our friend David Venable at QVC loves mac n' cheese and I think he would kick me off of the set if I didn't make it for him every time we visit! We wanted to come through with another great mac n' cheese recipe this go 'round and Nancy Kitts from Birmingham, Alabama, was our hero. She is a caterer, recipe developer, food stylist and one of the sweetest ladies I've ever met. Her recipe is creamy, cheesy and topped with a cracker crust that adds a crunch to each bite. Her recipe also passed the ultimate taste test and won our kid's approval! I can't wait to share this recipe with our friend David – and everyone else we know!

NANCY'S SMOKED MAC & CHEESE
Serves 6

You'll Need

- 1 (8 ounce) package elbow macaroni

- 1 teaspoon extra virgin olive oil

- 4 ounce Velveeta Cheese, grated

- 4 cups sharp Cheddar cheese, grated

- 1 cup sour cream

- 1 cup Hellmann's mayonnaise

- 1 1/2 teaspoons onion powder

- 1/2 teaspoon Cajun seasoning

- 1 1/2 cups crushed cheese crackers

Instructions

1. Preheat smoker to 275°F.

2. Cook macaroni according to package directions, adding olive oil to the water before boiling to avoid sticking. Drain and rinse with warm water. Add Velveeta and Cheddar cheeses, sour cream, mayonnaise, onion powder and Cajun seasoning, and stir together well.

3. Place mixture in a greased 11- by 7-inch disposable aluminum foil pan, and top with crushed cheese crackers. Place in smoker and smoke for 1 hour. Remove from smoker and enjoy.

4. Add wood chips the last 10 to 15 minutes of cooking time (do not over smoke).

❯ suggested wood
HICKORY

(It's not necessary to use wood chips if your smoker is well seasoned, and you would like a lighter smoke flavor.)

BRINED CHICKEN QUARTERS
Serves 4

This recipe benefits from two processes for the ultimate taste and texture. First, brining the chicken hydrates the meat and ensures a juicy result. Second, the smoking process infuses smokey flavor into the meat. Combining the seasonings and moisture from the brine with the low-and-slow smoking process makes for a perfect piece of chicken! Brushing the chicken quarters with olive oil helps the skin turn a nice golden brown.

Instructions

1.   In a large stockpot over medium heat, combine 2 cups water, molasses and salt. Bring to a boil until salt is dissolved. Remove from heat and stir in soy sauce, Worcestershire sauce, ginger and garlic powder. Set aside and let cool.

2.   When mixture is cooled, stir in 2 gallons ice water, mixing well. Place each chicken quarter in a brining bag or oversized plastic bag. Pour brining mixture over each chicken quarter and place in a bowl. Refrigerate, turning once, for 6 to 8 hours. A plastic bucket that is deep enough to have the meat completely covered will also work.

3.   Preheat smoker to 225°F. Remove meat from brine, after at least 6 hours, and rinse thoroughly to remove any remaining salt. Pat dry and brush with olive oil. Place on middle rack of smoker and smoke for 3 to 3 1/2 hours or until internal temperature reaches 165°F. Remove meat from smoker and enjoy!

You'll Need

- 2 cups water
- 2 cups molasses
- 2 cups kosher salt
- 1/4 cup soy sauce
- 2 tablespoons Worcestershire sauce
- 1/2 teaspoon freshly grated peeled ginger root
- 1/4 teaspoon garlic powder
- 2 gallons ice water
- 4 chicken quarters
- 2 tablespoons extra virgin olive oil

Brine Optional
We recommend using our "DADGUM That's Good!"™ Brine (page 13) as another option to the brining ingredients listed in Step 1.

❯ suggested wood
APPLE

PORK TENDERLOINS WITH PEACH SAUCE
Serves 4 to 6

My wife, Tonya, loves snacks that are salty and sweet. This recipe satisfies that salty-sweet craving in a main dish. Wrapping the tenderloin in bacon eliminates the need to wrap it in foil and adds great flavor. The peach sauce is the perfect finishing touch on the tenderloin slices. I would suggest serving over rice.

You'll Need

- 1 package pork tenderloins (contains 2)
- 8 slices bacon
- 1 tablespoon Jane's Krazy Mixed-Up Salt
- 2 (each 16-ounce) jars peach jam
- 5 tablespoons teriyaki sauce or General Tso's Sauce
- 1 cup water
- 1 cup thinly sliced green onions, green parts only
- 1 1/2 tablespoons all-purpose flour

Instructions

1. Wrap tenderloins with bacon slices and season sparingly with Krazy salt. Place meat in a large disposable aluminum foil pan.

2. In a small saucepan over low heat, combine peach jam, teriyaki sauce, water and green onions. Bring to a slow boil, stirring constantly until mixed well. Reserve 1 cup of marinade for later. Pour remaining marinade over tenderloins and marinate in the refrigerator, turning halfway through, for 1 1/2 hours.

3. Preheat smoker to 250°F. Place tenderloins on lower rack of smoker and smoke for 2 1/2 to 3 hours or until internal temperature reaches 160°F. Pour reserved 1 cup of marinade into a small skillet. Heat over medium heat and stir in all-purpose flour until thickened. Pour over tenderloins and serve.

▶ suggested wood
HICKORY

My wife Tonya's father was named Wes. Tonya and Wes ordered a food dehydrator from QVC one day and made beef jerky together. It was a fun project for them and we later gave Wes an electric Masterbuilt smoker so he could smoke jerky. He lived just down the street from us and had a great friendship with my dad, Dawson. Wes challenged me on smoked ribs a time or two and I won, but I never could beat his beef jerky. Wes passed away in 2010 and we've missed having him around. He was a great father-in-law and a great man. He raised the best dadgum good girl I've ever known, and for that I'll be eternally grateful.

Top Left: *Walking his baby girl down the aisle.*
Top Right: *Dawson and Wes were best buds.*
Middle: *Watermelon eating contest!*
Bottom: *Tonya was definitely a daddy's girl.*

WES' BEEF JERKY

Serves 6 to 8

Instructions

1. Have roast sliced into 1/4-inch strips when you purchase it. In a small saucepan over medium heat, combine vinegar, kosher salt, brown sugar, molasses, hot sauce and onion powder. Bring to a boil. Reduce heat and stir well. Remove from heat and let cool. Add 1 can of Coca-Cola.

2. Stack strips in a 10-inch square pan and pour marinade over each layer. Cover and refrigerate. Marinate for at least 4 hours, turning once, if not completely covered with marinade. Remove from marinade and pat dry. Place in a disposable aluminum foil pan.

3. Preheat smoker to 180°F. Fill water pan with remaining can of Coca Cola, 1/2 cup water and 2 tablespoons minced garlic. Sprinkle generously with Jane's Krazy salt and place on middle and top racks in smoker. Do not let strips touch. Smoke for at least 3 1/2 to 4 hours, checking for doneness and dryness after 3 1/2 hours, or until internal temperature reaches 145°F. If not ready, continue smoking for another 30 minutes, until meat is a dark color inside and out.

4. Let cool. Place in a resealable bag and refrigerate for several hours or freeze for up to 3 months or until ready to eat.

You'll Need

- 2 sirloin tip roasts (each about 1 pound), cut into 1/4-inch strips

- 1 cup apple cider vinegar

- 2 tablespoons kosher salt

- 2 tablespoons packed dark brown sugar

- 2 tablespoons molasses

- 1 tablespoon hot sauce (your favorite brand)

- 1 teaspoon onion powder

- 2 (each 7 1/2-ounce) cans Coca Cola, divided

- 2 tablespoons minced garlic

- Jane's Krazy Mixed-Up Salt

▶ **suggested wood**
APPLE

You'll Need

- 1 can ginger ale

- 1 fresh or frozen whole chicken (4 to 5 pounds), thawed if frozen

- 2 tablespoons + 1/2 teaspoon "DADGUM That's Good!"™ Seasoning (page 12)

- Butterball Buttery Creole Injection Marinade or your favorite marinade

DADGUM GOOD SMOKED CHICKEN

Serves 3 to 4

We have a lot of chicken recipes in this cookbook. In fact, we even wondered for a minute or so if we had too many. But honestly, you can't have too many chicken recipes in a cookbook! Think about it — how many times have you been looking for yet another way to prepare chicken?! It's an inexpensive choice of meat and there are countless ways to add flavor. You'll be hard-pressed to find a method that lends a juicier result than low-and-slow smoking. Remember to monitor the internal temp of this chicken carefully; it's ready for the dinner table when it reaches 165°F.

Instructions

1. Preheat smoker to 250°F. Fill water tray 1/2 full with water, then add 1 can ginger ale.

2. Rinse chicken and pat dry. Rub with 2 tablespoons of the seasoning and using a marinade injection syringe, inject 1 tablespoon marinade into each breast and 1 teaspoon into each leg and thigh. Place on middle rack of smoker and smoke for 1 1/2 to 3 hours or until internal temperature reaches 165°F. Remove and sprinkle with remaining 1/2 teaspoon of seasoning. Enjoy with your favorite veggies!

▶ suggested wood
HICKORY

Dry Rub

- 1/2 cup paprika
- 4 tablespoons garlic powder
- 4 tablespoons onion powder
- 2 1/2 tablespoons dried oregano
- 2 1/2 tablespoons kosher salt
- 1 tablespoon freshly ground black pepper
- 1 tablespoon cayenne pepper

- 1 beef brisket (about 5 pounds)

DADGUM GOOD BRISKET
Serves 4 to 6

Our food stylist at QVC, Nick, shared a couple of great recipes with us for this cookbook (Nick's Smoked Prime Rib). He's so much more than a food stylist. In addition to making the food look good, he makes it taste dadgum good! I've enjoyed spending time with him in the test kitchen and learning some of his tricks of the trade. Every time we smoke a brisket at QVC, it turns out perfect. He shared his dry rub recipe for this brisket and got our DTG seal of approval.

Instructions

1. **Dry Rub:** In a medium bowl, combine paprika, garlic powder, onion powder, oregano, salt, black pepper and cayenne pepper.

2. Preheat smoker to 250°F.

3. Coat beef brisket evenly with dry rub mixture. Place brisket on middle rack of smoker and smoke for 3 to 5 hours or until internal temperature reaches 180°F. Check internal temperature halfway through smoking.

❯ suggested wood
HICKORY

Top: Me and Tonya with the Governor at Fox News.

Middle: Tonya and her best friend Alicia with the Governor.

Bottom: Thumbs-up with the Governor!

GOVERNOR HUCKABEE'S SMOKED TENDERLOIN
Serves 10 to 12

In 2008, I met Governor Huckabee in NYC when I was deep frying turkey for "Fox and Friends." He fell in love with our deep-fried turkey and we formed an instant friendship. He's a big fan of Masterbuilt's electric turkey fryer and electric smoker. We've had the privilege of being on his show on Fox twice and it's always good to see him. The Governor is an awesome cook and I'm proud to feature his smoked tenderloin recipe in this book. The recipe and the Governor get our "thumbs up!"

Instructions

1. Remove the fat "chain," and all membrane and silver skin from tenderloin. (You can also ask your butcher to do this for you.)

2. Fold thin end of tenderloin under so thickness is even, then tie with butcher's string in 6 to 8 places.

3. Sprinkle tenderloin with kosher salt. Wrap in plastic wrap or foil and let stand at room temperature for 1 hour. Remove plastic wrap and apply a thin coat of olive oil and sprinkle with freshly cracked black peppercorns.

4. Preheat smoker to 225°F to 250°F. Place tenderloin in smoker and smoke for 55 to 65 minutes or until the internal temperature registers 120°F to 125°F for rare to medium-rare or 130°F to 135°F for medium-rare to medium. Cooking times can vary a lot and this is an expensive piece of meat! Don't go by time — use a meat temperature probe and trust it more than the clock.

5. After tenderloin has smoked to desired temperature and doneness, an option worth doing is to sear tenderloin on all four sides. Place on a very hot grill for about 2 minutes per side. This will give the outside a slight caramelized crust. I know that most of the time with beef (such as steaks) you sear it first, then cook it. Do the opposite with the tenderloin — smoke it first and THEN sear it at the end.

6. Cover loosely with foil and let rest for 10 minutes before slicing. This is when you DO want to use the clock! Don't rush it! Let those dadgum good juices settle before you go slicing into it.

You'll Need

- 1 whole beef tenderloin (4 to 6 pounds)
- Kosher salt
- Extra virgin olive oil to coat
- Freshly cracked black peppercorns

▶ suggested wood
APPLE OR HICKORY

SMOKED PORK LOIN ROAST
Serves 6 to 8

When wrapping this pork loin roast, make a "boat" with heavy-duty aluminum foil. Stack three long sheets of aluminum foil together. Place the roast in the middle of the foil and gather both of the long ends at the top. Roll those ends down toward the roast together. Fold up the sides and seal tightly. By using this method, instead of rolling the roast in foil, you contain the juices and avoid spilling them when you unwrap the roast at the end of the grilling process. Slice and serve with the sautéed onions.

Instructions

1. Randomly cut 5 slits about 1/2 inch deep into roast. Place a clove of garlic in each slit, along with a peppercorn. Place roast in an 8-inch square disposable aluminum foil pan and pour soy sauce over to cover at least half of roast. Marinate in refrigerator for at least 2 hours, turning after 1 hour to cover the other side of the roast.

2. Preheat smoker to 200°F.

3. In a medium skillet, heat olive oil over medium heat. Add onions and cook, stirring frequently until onions are beginning to brown. Set aside.

4. Remove pork loin from marinade, discarding marinade. Place on middle rack of smoker and smoke for 2 hours. Remove and wrap with heavy-duty aluminum foil. Return to smoker and smoke for an additional 2 hours or until internal temperature reaches 170°F.

5. Remove meat from smoker. Discard garlic and peppercorns and top with cracked pepper and reserved onions. Let roast rest for 5 to 10 minutes before slicing. Slice and serve.

You'll Need

- 1 rib end pork loin roast (3 to 4 pounds)
- 5 cloves garlic
- 5 whole black peppercorns
- 1 (10-ounce) bottle soy sauce
- 2 tablespoons extra virgin olive oil
- 1 large yellow onion, cut into rings
- 1/4 teaspoon cracked black peppercorns

❱ suggested wood
MESQUITE

BRINED WHOLE TURKEY
Serves 8 to 10

I'm a big fan of injection marinades. Not just because we make marinades, but more for the benefit of accelerating the process of adding flavor to meat. However, I've come to appreciate the brining process while writing this book. If you've got the time, brining is a fantastic way to prepare your turkey and it lends to a juicy result every time. I keep a Styrofoam cooler handy in my garage for this process. Lining it with a heavy-duty trash bag helps, as well. Try this recipe our way the first time, then don't be shy about changing up the spices and making it your own.

Instructions

1. Brine turkey according to instructions on page 13 for 12 hours. If the turkey is not completely covered, turn once during brining. Do not leave the turkey in the brine longer than 12 hours.

2. Preheat smoker to 225°F.

3. Remove turkey from brine and rinse well inside and out to avoid being too salty after cooking. This is a very important step. After thoroughly rinsing all salt off, pat dry. Baste turkey with olive oil. Cover the wings and drumsticks halfway through smoking so they don't burn, and place foil over the breasts once they reach 150°F so they're not overcooked when the rest of the turkey is done.

4. Place turkey on middle rack of smoker and smoke for 5 to 6 hours or 30 to 35 minutes per pound or until the internal temperature reaches 165°F.

You'll Need

- "DADGUM That's Good!"™ Brine (page 13)

- 1 fresh or frozen turkey (about 10 pounds), thawed if frozen

- 1/4 cup extra virgin olive oil

▶ suggested wood
MESQUITE

DADGUM GOOD GUMBO
Serves 8 to 10

The beauty of this Dadgum Good Gumbo is that you can truly make it your own. It calls for smoked chicken and turkey sausage, but we have served it up with pork sausage, kielbasa or shrimp (precooked or raw). If you're looking for a dish that freezes well, this is the one. Freeze in gallon-size resealable baggies and let thaw in hot water, then reheat on low in a large pot.

Instructions

1. Preheat smoker to 250°F.

2. Pierce each half of the chicken with a fork. Baste each with 1 tablespoon olive oil. Sprinkle 1/4 teaspoon meat tenderizer on each. Place chicken on middle rack of smoker and smoke for 2 to 3 1/2 hours or until internal temperature reaches 165°F.

3. Meanwhile, in a large stockpot, prepare gumbo mix according to package directions. Stir in celery, okra, garlic, green onions, sweet onion and liquid shrimp boil, combining well. Bring to a boil. Reduce heat to medium-low and simmer, covered, for 15 minutes.

4. When chicken is finished cooking, let cool and pull meat from bone. Slice turkey sausage into 1/4-inch slices. Add both chicken and sausage to gumbo and simmer on low for 20 minutes. Add uncooked rice, stir well, and simmer on low for another 15 minutes. If rice needs additional cooking, turn heat off, leave pot covered, and let stand until rice is ready. If you prefer the gumbo to be thinner, add a small amount of water and stir well. Enjoy this delicious gumbo with your favorite bread or crackers!

You'll Need

- 1 roaster chicken, split (about 4 pounds)
- 2 tablespoons extra virgin olive oil, divided
- 1/2 teaspoon meat tenderizer, divided
- 2 (each 5-ounce) packages Louisiana fish fry gumbo mix
- 1 cup sliced celery
- 1 3/4 cups sliced okra
- 2 teaspoons minced garlic
- 1/2 cup thinly sliced green onions, green parts only
- 1/2 cup chopped sweet onion
- 1 teaspoon liquid shrimp boil
- 1 pound turkey sausage
- 1 cup uncooked rice (your favorite type)
- French bread or crackers

▶ suggested wood
MESQUITE

SMOKED BOSTON BUTT
Serves 4 to 6

When preparing Boston butts, folks naturally migrate toward dry rub seasonings or marinades. The method of injecting marinade works so well with poultry that I tried it with a Boston butt at home one day and was blown away with the results. Injection marinades are a quick way to add flavor to your meat. Some people even call this method "accelerated brining." If you make several of these Boston butts at one time, you can freeze them for later meals. Wrap them in heavy-duty aluminum foil before freezing. Thaw them later and place back on the smoker, grill or oven for an hour or so, in the foil, to warm before serving.

Instructions

1. Preheat smoker to 225°F.

2. Place butt in a large bowl. Using a marinade injection syringe, inject 8 ounces of steak marinade into butt (1 ounce at a time in several locations throughout the butt). Reserve remaining 4 ounces of marinade for basting later.

3. Place butt on the middle rack of smoker and smoke, basting every hour, for 6 hours or until internal temperature reaches 165°F.

You'll Need

- 1 pork butt (4 to 5 pounds)

- 1 (12-ounce) steak marinade, such as Dale's or Moore's, or your favorite dark steak marinade

❯ suggested wood
HICKORY

SMOKED LIMA BEANS WITH HAM

Serves 6 to 8

This recipe takes some time, but it's more than worth it. The longer you cook the beans, the better they taste. You will notice that the instructions call for only 30 minutes of smoking time before you wrap this dish. Vegetables have a tendency to absorb smoke quickly and intensely, so you need to be careful not to oversmoke them. You can pair these with many of the smoked meat recipes on these pages, or just eat a big bowl of lima beans for the ultimate comfort meal.

Instructions

1. Preheat smoker to 225°F.

2. Place beans in a Dutch oven with 8 cups of water. Bring to a boil and boil for 3 minutes. Let beans soak, covered, for 1 hour. Rinse beans well and add 6 1/4 cups of fresh water and ham chunks. Bring this mixture to a boil and remove from heat.

3. Place beans in a deep-dish round disposable aluminum foil pan; you may need to pour a small amount of liquid out. Place on middle rack of smoker and smoke for 30 minutes. Remove pan and cover with heavy-duty aluminum foil. Return to smoker and smoke for an additional 7 1/2 hours. Check for desired tenderness, and return to smoker if needed. When the beans are done, remove and add salt and pepper.

You'll Need

- 1 (2-pound) package dried lima beans

- 14 1/4 cups water, divided

- 2 (each 16-ounce) packages ham chunks

- 1 teaspoon salt

- 1/4 teaspoon cracked black pepper

▶ suggested wood
HICKORY

DARRYL'S BOSTON BUTT

Serves 6 to 8

Our employee events and celebrations at Masterbuilt give our folks the opportunity to show off their skills at the grill or smoker. When we hosted a dinner for the Fishers of Men, a local organization for Christian fishermen, Darryl (Senior Quality Engineer) smoked Boston butts. I was so impressed with the results, I knew we had to put his recipe in the book. It's awesome to work with so many amateur chefs when you manufacture cooking products. Another option with this recipe is to increase the smoker temp to 275°F at the end, unwrap the butt, and place back in the smoker for an additional 30 to 45 minutes to form a hard crust/bark. Remove and let rest before pulling. A mustard-based BBQ sauce makes the perfect finishing touch.

Instructions

1. Season pork butt generously with dry rub seasoning. Place pork in a resealable plastic bag. Spread mustard evenly over butt while inside the bag to avoid mess. Seal bag and refrigerate overnight.

2. Preheat smoker to 225°F.

3. Place butt on middle rack of smoker and smoke for 7 to 8 hours or until internal temperature reaches 185°F. Remove from smoker. Cover with heavy-duty aluminum foil and return to smoker. Increase smoker temperature to 275°F. Smoke for an additional 2 hours or until internal temperature reaches 200°F. Let meat rest inside foil for 30 minutes. Then pull pork.

You'll Need

- 1 pork butt (8 pounds)

- 4 tablespoons "DADGUM That's Good!"™ Dry Rub (page 12)

- 6 to 7 heaping tablespoons yellow mustard

▶ suggested wood
HICKORY

Darryl is camera shy, but Danny from Masterbuilt isn't! We served up Darryl's Boston Butt at his Fishers of Men dinner at Masterbuilt.

One of the highlights of my first book tour was our visits to the "700 Club." There are truly some fantastic and genuine folks on the "700 Club" team and we had an amazing time working with them. I've had the pleasure of working with Terry and Kristi on cooking segments and enjoyed meeting Pat and Gordon Robertson. They loved our food so much that Kristi even asked my wife if she could take me home! Although I'm sure the good folks at the "700 Club" didn't really want to take me home, they did send Gordon's recipe for Persian Lamb home with me.

Top Left: *With Terry, host of the "700 Club."*
Top Right: *Kristi, Tonya, Pat and me at the "700 Club."*
Bottom: *Kristi loved our food!*

GORDON'S PERSIAN LAMB
Serves 4 to 6

Instructions

1. In a spice grinder or clean coffee grinder, grind coriander, pepper, cumin and cardamom until well combined.

2. Remove bone and butterfly the leg of lamb. (You can also ask your butcher to do this for you.) Place lamb flat on the kitchen counter or cutting board with the meaty side facing up and the fatty side facing down. (This way, when the roast is rolled, the fat will be on the outside, basting the meat throughout cooking. You may need to pound a few areas with a meat mallet to uniformly flatten the lamb as much as possible.) Let meat rest for 20 minutes to soften and come to room temperature.

3. Rub spice mix into both sides of meat and sprinkle with sea salt. Roll lamb up tightly and tie with moistened kitchen twine. Place in a large bowl. Pour pomegranate juice over lamb. Cover bowl tightly with plastic wrap and refrigerate, turning halfway through, for 6 to 10 hours or overnight.

4. Preheat smoker to 275°F.

5. **Pomegranate Molasses (if using):** In a saucepan over medium heat, combine pomegranate juice, sugar and orange juice. Cook, stirring occasionally, until sugar is completely dissolved. Reduce heat to medium-low and cook, stirring occasionally, until mixture is reduced to 1 cup, about 90 minutes. (It should be the consistency of thick syrup and coat the back of a wooden spoon well.) Remove from heat and let thicken in saucepan for 30 minutes. Serve in a sauceboat or directly from the saucepan with a spoon. Transfer leftover molasses to a glass jar and allow it to cool completely. It can be stored in the refrigerator for up to 6 months. Also good as a sauce for chicken or pork.

6. Remove lamb from marinade, discarding marinade. Place lamb on smoker rack. Insert a meat thermometer into the thickest portion of the lamb and place on middle rack in smoker. Smoke lamb for 1 1/2 to 2 1/2 hours for medium-rare to medium or until thermometer registers 145°F. Remove roast from smoker and let rest at room temperature for 15 minutes before carving to allow meat to reabsorb the juices. The residual heat will raise the roast's temperature to 150°F. Remove twine. Serve with Pomegranate Molasses, if using.

You'll Need

- 1 tablespoon ground coriander
- 1 tablespoon freshly ground black pepper
- 1 1/2 teaspoons ground cumin
- 10 pods cardamom (or 1 1/2 teaspoons ground)
- 1 (4-pound) boneless leg of lamb
- Sea salt
- 1 cup pomegranate juice

Pomegranate Molasses (optional)

- 4 cups pomegranate juice
- 1/2 cup granulated sugar
- 1 tablespoon freshly squeezed orange juice

❱ suggested wood
APPLE OR HICKORY

SMOKED BABY BACK RIBS WITH BBQ SAUCE

Serves 4 to 5

To wrap or not to wrap? That is the question most asked when smoking ribs or pork butt. I use both methods, but prefer to wrap. With this recipe, you get the best of both methods. They are left unwrapped long enough to absorb smokey flavor, then wrapped in foil with BBQ sauce to get that fall-off-the-bone result. The last step of returning to the smoker for 30 minutes unwrapped is critical, as it gives the ribs a great finishing texture. Warning: These ribs are dadgum messy. Who cares, as long as they are dadgum good?!

Instructions

1. Preheat smoker to 225°F.

2. Sprinkle ribs generously with lime pepper and Krazy salt. Place on middle rack of smoker and smoke, uncovered, for 2 hours.

3. BBQ Sauce: Meanwhile, in a heavy saucepan over low heat, combine ketchup, cider vinegar, lemon juice, garlic powder, onion powder and garlic pepper and stir well. Simmer, stirring occasionally, for 10 to 15 minutes.

4. Remove ribs from smoker and wrap in aluminum foil. Return to smoker and smoke for an additional 2 hours. Remove from smoker, baste with BBQ sauce and return to smoker, unwrapped, for an additional 30 minutes or until internal temperature reaches 165°F. Serve remaining sauce on the side.

You'll Need

- 2 slabs baby back ribs
- Lime pepper
- Jane's Krazy Mixed-Up Salt

BBQ Sauce

- 2 cups ketchup
- 1/4 cup apple cider vinegar
- 2 tablespoons fresh lemon juice
- 1 teaspoon garlic powder
- 1 teaspoon onion powder
- 1 teaspoon garlic pepper

❱ suggested wood
APPLE

SMOKED CHICKEN TENDERS
Serves 6 to 8

You may have already enjoyed my daughter Bailey's fried chicken fingers with honey mustard sauce, which goes well with these. The kids and teens that hang around our home love these. For the adults, who are a bit more concerned about their waistline, these smoked chicken tenders provide a lighter alternative. The honey mustard sauce on (page 107) goes well with these tenders, also.

Instructions

1. In a medium bowl, combine soy sauce, vegetable oil, water, sesame seeds, garlic, ginger, Cajun seasoning and 1/2 teaspoon Jane's Krazy salt, and mix well. Place tenders in a resealable plastic bag, pour marinade over tenders and seal. Refrigerate for 8 hours or overnight. Turn bag at least two times to make sure all meat is well marinated.

2. When ready to smoke, preheat smoker to 225°F.

3. Remove tenders from marinade, discarding marinade. Place tenders carefully on the middle rack of smoker and smoke for 45 minutes to 1 hour or until internal temperature reaches 165°F. Sprinkle to taste with Jane's Krazy salt.

You'll Need

- 1/2 cup soy sauce
- 1/2 cup vegetable oil
- 1/4 cup water
- 1 1/2 tablespoons sesame seeds
- 2 teaspoons minced garlic
- 3/4 teaspoon freshly grated peeled ginger root
- 1/4 teaspoon Cajun seasoning
- Jane's Krazy Mixed-Up Salt
- 4 pounds chicken tenders, rinsed and patted dry

❯ suggested wood
HICKORY

SMOKEY PIMENTO CHEESE DIP
Serves 16

This recipe is awesome as a stand-alone dish, but we make it even more awesome by pairing it with two other dishes in this book. You can use this for the Christy's Smoked Pimento Cheese Appetizer on page 57 or the Fried Pimento Cheese Balls on page 108. If you use this dip for the Fried Pimento Cheese Balls, make sure you place it in the freezer for an hour or so to firm up before forming the balls. I highly recommend serving this dip with Frito Scoop chips

Instructions

1. Preheat smoker to 225°F.

2. In a medium bowl, combine Cheddar cheese, Colby Jack cheese, cream cheese and Alouette cheese spread, mixing well. Add mayonnaise, green onions, pepper and pimento. Mix until creamy. Place in an 8-inch square baking dish or a disposable aluminum foil pan.

3. Place on middle rack of smoker and smoke for 20 minutes. Remove and serve immediately with corn chips, soft French bread cubes or bagel chips.

You'll Need

- 1 (16-ounce) block sharp Cheddar cheese, grated

- 1 (8-ounce) block Colby Jack cheese, grated

- 4 ounces cream cheese, softened

- 1/4 cup Alouette Sun-Dried Tomato and Basil cheese spread or your favorite variety

- 3/4 cup mayonnaise

- 1/4 cup thinly sliced green onions, green parts only

- 1/4 teaspoon coarsely ground black pepper

- 1 large (4-ounce) jar pimento, diced and drained

- Corn chips, French bread cubes and/or bagel chips

▶ suggested wood
HICKORY

In the past several years, we have worked with food bloggers on several projects with Masterbuilt and I've enjoyed spending time with them during our travels. One of those bloggers who has become a friend is Christy Jordan of Southern Plate. She's a down-to-earth Southern lady who instantly connected with our team. Within minutes of meeting one another, we were talking recipes. When she shared her recipe for Smoked Pimento Cheese and Cracker Appetizers, she was speaking my language. Honestly, anything with smoked sausage is good in my book, but pairing it with pimento cheese and jalapeños turns good into dadgum good!

Top and Bottom: Christy hanging out with our team at a food blogging conference.
Middle: Me and my new friend Christy.

CHRISTY'S SMOKED PIMENTO CHEESE APPETIZER

Serves 8 to 10

Instructions

1. Preheat smoker to 225°F.

2. Smoke sausage for 45 minutes to 1 hour. Remove from smoker.

3. Place saltine crackers on a platter, salt-side down. Place 1 teaspoon of pimento cheese spread on each cracker. Slice smoked sausage in 1/2-inch sections and place each slice on top of pimento spread while still warm. Top each with 1 jalapeño slice. Serve immediately.

You'll Need

- 1 pound kielbasa sausage

- Saltine crackers

- Smokey Pimento Cheese Dip (page 55) or 1 (12-ounce) container of your favorite pimento cheese spread

- Sliced jalapeño peppers

▶ suggested wood

HICKORY

SMOKED SHRIMP PO' BOYS WITH RÉMOULADE SAUCE

Serves 6

When people think of shrimp po' boys, they think of New Orleans. I think of Alabama. The University of Alabama football team, to be specific. Why, might you ask? The BCS National Title Game was played in New Orleans in 2012, between the Alabama Crimson Tide and the LSU Tigers. We had a viewing party at our house after a long day of recipe testing and served up these shrimp po' boy sandwiches. The recipe and the Tide kicked butt that night!

Instructions

1. In water tray, add liquid shrimp boil, bay leaves and water. Preheat smoker to 250°F.

2. Place shrimp in a 13- by 9-inch baking dish or a disposable aluminum foil pan and drizzle with lemon juice. In a small saucepan over medium heat, melt butter. Add Worcestershire sauce, Cajun seasoning and garlic pepper, mixing well. Pour over shrimp.

3. Place shrimp on middle rack of smoker, uncovered. Reduce smoker to 225°F and smoke for about 50 minutes. Remove from smoker and place under oven broiler to broil shrimp to lightly brown, about 3 minutes.

4. Rémoulade Sauce: In a food processor, combine oil, mayonnaise, mustard, horseradish, lemon juice, parsley, red wine vinegar, paprika and garlic and purée until smooth

5. Spread Rémoulade sauce over each side of buns. Place shredded lettuce on each, several slices of tomato and dill slices. Mound shrimp on each sandwich and enjoy!

You'll Need

- 4 tablespoons liquid shrimp boil
- 3 bay leaves
- 1/2 cup water
- 4 pounds large shrimp, peeled, deveined and washed
- Juice of 3 lemons
- 1/2 cup butter
- 1 tablespoon Worcestershire sauce
- 1 tablespoon Cajun seasoning
- 1 tablespoon garlic pepper
- 6 po' boy buns, or French bread, cut to desired size
- 3 cups shredded iceberg lettuce, shredded
- 3 large tomatoes, thinly sliced
- 2 cups thinly sliced dill pickles

Rémoulade Sauce

- 1/4 cup vegetable oil
- 1/4 cup mayonnaise
- 2 tablespoons Creole mustard
- 2 tablespoons horseradish sauce
- 2 tablespoons fresh lemon juice
- 1 tablespoon fresh parsley
- 2 teaspoons red wine vinegar
- 1 teaspoon paprika
- 2 1/2 teaspoons minced fresh garlic

▶ suggested wood
MESQUITE

SMOKED CORNED BEEF WITH POTATOES AND ONIONS

Serves 4 to 6

This recipe stands well on its own as a complete meal. Another great option is to use the leftover corned beef to make Reuben sandwiches. Slice the meat and serve on toasted sourdough bread with sauerkraut. On St. Patrick's Day at Masterbuilt we had an employee event and served up Reuben sandwiches. I love my team at Masterbuilt because they don't do anything halfway. They went all-out with the theme, décor and menu. Our Marketing Director even dressed as a leprechaun (see page 80) and danced around the conference room. I'm pretty dadgum proud that my team knows how to work hard and play hard!

Instructions

1. Discard liquid in brisket bag. Place brisket in a deep 12-inch square disposable aluminum foil pan. Pour Coca Cola over and add spice packet. (If spice packet is missing increase pickling spice to 6 tablespoons.) Add 2 garlic cloves and 1 tablespoon of pickling spices. Cover with aluminum foil and refrigerate, turning once, for 3 hours.

2. Fill water pan and add bay leaves, remaining 4 garlic cloves and remaining 3 tablespoons pickling spice. Preheat smoker to 250°F.

3. Wash potatoes well and place potatoes, with skins on, and onion in a disposable aluminum foil pan. Drizzle with olive oil and sprinkle with sea salt. Cover with aluminum foil. Place on top rack of smoker and smoke for the last hour of smoking brisket.

4. Place brisket pan, covered with foil, on middle rack of smoker. Reduce smoker temperature to 225°F. Smoke for 4 1/2 to 5 hours or until internal temperature reaches 160°F. Remove brisket and unwrap foil. Return brisket to smoker and cook for an additional 30 minutes. Remove brisket and potatoes and onions from smoker. Slice brisket and serve with potatoes and onions.

You'll Need

- 1 corned beef brisket (3 to 4 pounds), with spice packet
- 1 (7 1/2-ounce) can Coca Cola
- 6 cloves garlic, divided
- 4 tablespoons pickling spices, divided
- 5 bay leaves
- 1 1/2 pounds tiny golden potatoes
- 1 large onion, coarsely chopped
- 2 tablespoons extra virgin olive oil
- 2 teaspoons sea salt

▶ **suggested wood**
HICKORY

SMOKED CHICKEN SALAD SANDWICHES
Serves 8

Folks in the South love chicken salad. There are so many different variations of chicken salad and you'd most likely find it on the menu at a baby or wedding shower! Well, once you taste this Smoked Chicken Salad, you won't want to wait for a birth or wedding to enjoy the goodness. You'll want it 7 days a week (and twice on some days!).

Instructions

1. Preheat smoker to 225°F. Fill water tray with water and add bay leaves.

2. Pierce chicken breasts with a fork and sprinkle with meat tenderizer. Place chicken on middle rack of smoker and smoke for 45 minutes per pound or until internal temperature reaches 165°F.

3. Meanwhile, place pecans in a small disposable aluminum foil pan, pour melted butter over top and sprinkle with kosher salt. Stir well to coat pecans. Place pan on top rack of smoker during the last half of smoking time for the chicken. Smoke pecans for 30 minutes. Remove from smoker and drain on a paper towel. Remove chicken. Let cool, then chop.

4. In a large bowl, combine chopped chicken, pecans, celery and dried cranberries. Add 1 1/3 cups mayonnaise. Season with Cajun seasoning, salt and pepper. (Add additional salt and pepper to suit your taste, if necessary.) Lightly spread each side of the buns with mayonnaise, and place a large leaf of red lettuce on the bottom half. Place a generous amount of chicken salad on top of lettuce and enjoy!

You'll Need

- 3 bay leaves
- 3 large boneless skinless chicken breasts
- 2 teaspoons meat tenderizer
- 3/4 cup pecans, very coarsely chopped
- 1/4 cup butter, melted
- 1/4 teaspoon kosher salt
- 1 cup finely chopped celery
- 1 (5-ounce) bag dried cranberries
- 1 1/3 cups mayonnaise (approx.)
- 1/4 teaspoon Cajun seasoning
- 1/2 teaspoon salt
- 1/2 teaspoon freshly ground black pepper
- 8 soft hoagie buns
- Red leaf lettuce

▶ suggested wood
HICKORY

SMOKED CORNISH HENS
Serves 6

This recipe also works well with pheasant or whole chickens. I was hunting pheasant in South Dakota one time and came prepared for the Icelandic-cold weather we were warned about. Our first day out, the temperature was in the mid-40s and it was actually a pleasant day. Reality set in the next morning when the temperature plummeted to 15-below zero with a wind chill of 30-below. The hunting trip was a success, but let's just say this Georgia boy was ready to get back home and warm!

Instructions

1. Preheat smoker to 225°F.

2. Molasses Glaze: In a medium saucepan over medium heat, combine molasses, teriyaki sauce, ginger and vinegar and cook for 3 minutes. Add 1 tablespoon cornstarch to thicken. If not thick enough, add another 1/2 tablespoon. Remove from heat and set aside until ready to use.

3. Drizzle lemon juice generously over each Cornish hen. Baste very lightly with olive oil, which will brown in the smoker. (Do not put much or the glaze will not stay on the hens.) Sprinkle 1/4 teaspoon salt and 1/8 teaspoon pepper on each hen. Tie legs together with cooking twine. Place on middle rack of smoker and smoke for 3 1/2 hours or until internal temperature reaches 165°F. Let rest for 5 to 10 minutes. Pour glaze over top.

You'll Need

Molasses Glaze

- 1/2 cup molasses
- 1/4 cup teriyaki sauce
- 1/4 teaspoon freshly grated peeled ginger root
- 2 tablespoons white wine vinegar
- 1 to 1 1/2 tablespoons cornstarch

- Juice of 2 lemons
- 6 Cornish game hens, rinsed thoroughly and patted dry (each 1 1/2 pounds)
- Extra virgin olive oil
- 1 1/2 teaspoons salt
- 3/4 teaspoon freshly ground black pepper

▶ suggested wood
APPLE

SMOKED SWEET POTATOES
Serves 8 to 16

You know a side dish recipe is dadgum good when you would serve it as the main dish, and even for dessert! These smoked sweet potatoes fit that bill. The recipe calls for slicing the potatoes in half to serve two people. For my hungry crowd, we serve one potato per person. Want to take them to the next level? Drizzle lightly with caramel sauce and add a few small marshmallows.

Instructions

1. Preheat smoker to 275°F.

2. Wash and scrub each sweet potato well. Baste each with 1 teaspoon of olive oil. Sprinkle outside of each potato with 1/2 teaspoon of sea salt. Place sweet potatoes in smoker and smoke for 1 hour. Remove from smoker, double-wrap each potato securely with heavy-duty aluminum foil and place back in smoker for an additional hour.

3. Remove potatoes from smoker and unwrap from foil. Slice potatoes in half and score flesh with a fork. Top each potato half with 1 tablespoon of butter, 1 tablespoon of brown sugar and 1 tablespoon of chopped pecans.

You'll Need

- 8 large sweet potatoes

- 2 1/3 tablespoons extra virgin olive oil

- 1 1/2 tablespoons sea salt

- 1 cup butter

- 1 cup packed dark brown sugar

- 1 cup smoked or toasted pecans, coarsely chopped

To smoke pecans: Place pecans in a disposable aluminum foil pan. Smoke at 225°F for 10 minutes.

❱ suggested wood
APPLE

BACON-WRAPPED SMOKED ASPARAGUS
Serves 6

When it comes to asparagus, folks like it every way from crisp to fork-tender. You can go either way with this recipe by adjusting your smoke time. I recommend shaving 30 minutes off of the total cooking time if you want a crisp result. In the McLemore house, we think bacon makes everything better and this recipe is no exception. The French dressing gives this dish a unique and tangy flavor.

Instructions

1. Wash asparagus and cut the bottom two inches off each stalk. Divide into 6 bundles. Wrap each bundle securely with a slice of bacon. Place in a 12-inch square disposable aluminum foil pan. Pour dressing over and cover with aluminum foil. Refrigerate and marinate for 4 hours.

2. Preheat smoker to 250°F.

3. Remove asparagus from refrigerator and discard 1/2 cup of marinade. Re-cover with aluminum foil and pierce foil with a fork in center and three other places.

4. Place pan on middle rack of smoker and smoke for 45 minutes. Asparagus should be fork-tender. Add one small handful of wood chips to smoker and smoke asparagus for an additional 45 minutes, if you prefer it to be more tender. Remove from marinade and serve.

You'll Need

- 1 1/2 pounds fresh asparagus
- 1/2 pound bacon
- 1 (16-ounce) bottle French dressing

◗ suggested wood
APPLE

SMOKED CORN CASSEROLE
Serves 8

One of the most popular smoked corn recipes is corn smoked in the husks. You get a hint of smokey flavor, but the husk keeps the smoke from overpowering the corn. When making this corn casserole, we recommend the same approach. Fifteen minutes of smoke is just enough, without overpowering the entire dish. This casserole pairs well with any of our smoked meat recipes.

Instructions

1. Preheat smoker to 250°F.

2. In a large bowl, combine cream-style and kernel corn, onion, bell pepper, green chiles and cheese. In a small bowl, beat eggs and then add to other ingredients. Stir in cornbread mix. Pour into a lightly greased 10-inch square disposable aluminum foil pan. Cover tightly with heavy-duty aluminum foil.

3. Place on middle rack of smoker and smoke for 1 hour and 15 minutes. Add more wood to smoker, then remove foil and smoke for an additional 15 minutes for a total cooking time of 1 hour and 30 minutes.

You'll Need

- 1 (20-ounce) package frozen yellow cream-style corn, thawed

- 1 (10-ounce) package frozen whole kernel corn, thawed

- 1 cup chopped yellow onion

- 1/3 cup chopped green bell pepper

- 1 (4-ounce) can green chiles, drained and chopped

- 1 3/4 cups shredded Pepper Jack cheese

- 3 large eggs

- 1 (7-ounce) package cornbread mix

▶ suggested wood
MESQUITE

CAJUN SMOKED CHICKEN
Serves 6

Leaving chicken breasts skinless allows the smokey flavor to penetrate the meat more easily, but you will notice that the outside of the breasts take on a dark brown, tough appearance. Don't let appearances fool you. When you slice into these chicken breasts, you will find them moist and flavorful. Timing on boneless breasts is more critical than chicken with the bone-in (or dark meat), so make sure you watch the time and monitor the internal temperature.

Instructions

1. Pierce each piece of chicken on both sides with a fork. Drizzle both sides well with olive oil and red wine vinegar. Sprinkle with 1/2 tablespoon of Cajun seasoning. Place chicken in a 1-gallon resealable plastic bag overnight or for at least 3 to 4 hours in the refrigerator. Remove from refrigerator and sprinkle with Krazy salt and remaining 1 tablespoon of Cajun seasoning.

2. Fill water pan with water and add sweet onion slices and liquid shrimp boil. Preheat smoker to 225°F. Place on lower rack of smoker and smoke for 45 minutes per pound or until the internal temperature reaches 165°F. Remove and serve whole or slice in strips and serve.

You'll Need

- 6 large boneless skinless chicken breasts
- 6 tablespoons extra virgin olive oil
- 6 tablespoons red wine vinegar
- 1 1/2 tablespoons Cajun seasoning, divided
- 1 tablespoon Jane's Krazy Mixed-Up Salt
- 1 large sweet onion, sliced
- 3 tablespoons liquid shrimp boil

❯ suggested wood
HICKORY

DADGUM GOOD SMOKED TURKEY
Serves 6 to 12

When asked if there was anything I would change about my first cookbook, *"DADGUM That's Good!"*™, I have two words for you: SMOKED TURKEY. There are times in life when you miss something really obvious, and not having a smoked whole turkey recipe in my first cookbook was one of those times. Every time we appear on QVC with our smokers, we smoke a turkey. When folks opened up the first cookbook, we definitely heard some feedback on not having a smoked turkey recipe. We heard you loud and clear and hope you enjoy this recipe. In fact, we almost put a smoked turkey on the front of this cookbook instead of my picture. Some would argue there's still a turkey on the cover!

Instructions

Option 1 (shorter cook time)

1. Fill water tray 1/2 full with a 50/50 mixture of apple juice and water. Preheat smoker to 275°F.

2. Rinse and dry the thawed turkey. Using a marinade injection syringe, inject turkey with one jar of Butterball Buttery Creole marinade. Season outside and inside of turkey with Butterball Cajun Seasoning, rubbing it into the skin.

3. Place turkey on middle rack in smoker and close the door. Smoke for 5 1/2 hours or until internal temperature in breast reaches 165°F. (This total cooking time is for a 19-pound whole turkey. Based on the weight of your turkey, you will need to adjust the total cooking time. Estimated time at 275°F is about 18 minutes per pound. Make sure your internal temperature in the breast reaches 165°F.)

Option 2 (longer cook time)

1. Fill water pan 1/3 full with a 50/50 mixture of apple juice and water. Preheat smoker to 225°F.

2. See Step 2 above.

3. Place turkey on middle rack in smoker and close the door. Smoke for 9 1/2 hours or until internal temperature in breast reaches 165°F. (This total cooking time is for a 19-pound whole turkey. Based on the weight of your turkey, you will need to adjust the total cooking time. Estimated time at 225°F is about 30 minutes per pound. Make sure your internal temperature in the breast reaches 165°F.)

You'll Need

- 50/50 mixture apple juice and water

- 1 whole turkey (about 19 pounds), thawed if frozen

- Butterball Buttery Creole Injection Marinade or your favorite marinade

- Butterball Cajun Seasoning or your favorite Cajun seasoning

- Seasonings and marinades (optional) (see below)

Additional Seasoning/ Marinade Options:

We highly recommend the Butterball Seasoning Kit with the Buttery Creole Marinade and Cajun Seasoning, but there are other options if you prefer a milder flavor. You can inject the turkey with the marinade of your choice or chicken broth. Season the outside and inside of the turkey with salt and pepper, rubbing it into the skin. Place 8 to 10 pats of butter underneath the skin. You can also tuck several bay leaves underneath the skin.

◗ suggested wood

HICKORY, MESQUITE, APPLE OR PECAN

SWEET 'N' SPICY SMOKED HAM
Serves 10 to 12

I've been asked, "Why do you smoke a precooked ham?" Although you aren't "cooking" the ham, this process infuses tons of extra smokey flavor and the extra ingredients add a burst of sweet 'n' spicy taste. You can cut this ham recipe into chunks and add to the Smoked Lima Beans with Ham recipe on page 47. Remember, the seasonings from this ham will change the flavor of that recipe, but in a dadgum good way.

Instructions

1.   Preheat smoker to 225°F.

2.   In a small bowl, combine honey, brown sugar and mustard and rub over entire ham. On top of backside of ham, score an area about 5 inches wide and 3 inches deep. Push whole cloves, if using, into this area. Using a marinade injection syringe, inject ham with 4 ounces of the Cajun butter marinade. Place in a deep disposable aluminum foil pan, and pour remaining 4 ounces of marinade in bottom of pan.

3.   Place pan on middle rack of smoker and smoke, uncovered, for 45 minutes. Remove from smoker and cover. Return to smoker and smoke for an additional hour or until internal temperature reaches 160°F. Remove from smoker, ladle some of the marinade over and slice. If the cloves are in the way, remove and slice remaining ham.

You'll Need

- 1/4 cup honey

- 1/4 cup packed dark brown sugar

- 1 tablespoon Dijon mustard

- 1 precooked butt portion ham (10 pounds)

- 2 tablespoons whole cloves, approx. (optional)

- 1 (8-ounce) Cajun butter marinade injection kit, divided

▶ suggested wood
HICKORY

Oink 'n' Gobble, QVC-style!

OINK 'N' GOBBLE
Instructions

For Oink 'n' Gobble use the Dadgum Good Smoked Turkey recipe on page 69 and the Sweet 'n' Spicy Smoked Ham recipe on page 70.

1. Fill water pan 1/2 full with a 50/50 mixture of apple juice and water. Preheat smoker to 225°F.

2. Follow the recipe instructions for Dadgum Good Smoked Turkey (page 69). Place the turkey in the smoker. Proceed to Step 3 when turkey is on the last hour and 45 minutes of cooking time.

3. Follow the instructions for Sweet 'n' Spicy Smoked Ham (page 70) and place ham above the turkey in the smoker. Smoke ham for 45 minutes, uncovered, and then cover with aluminum foil and smoke for an additional hour or until internal temperature reaches 160°F. For the Dadgum Good Smoked Turkey the internal temperature should reach 165°F.

It seems we're always feeding a large crowd at the McLemore house, and we're doing it all year long – not just during the holidays. I'm all about freeing up the oven and using my smoker to cook all of the meat. Making a ham and turkey at the same time is a great way to feed a large crowd and create tons of yummy leftovers for sandwiches and other dishes. You want the ham above the turkey so that the juices drip down and add flavor. You can use any recipe you choose with this method, just make sure the poultry is below the ham. Oh, and when they are just about done, how about giving us a call so we can come over for dinner?!

❱ **suggested wood**
HICKORY

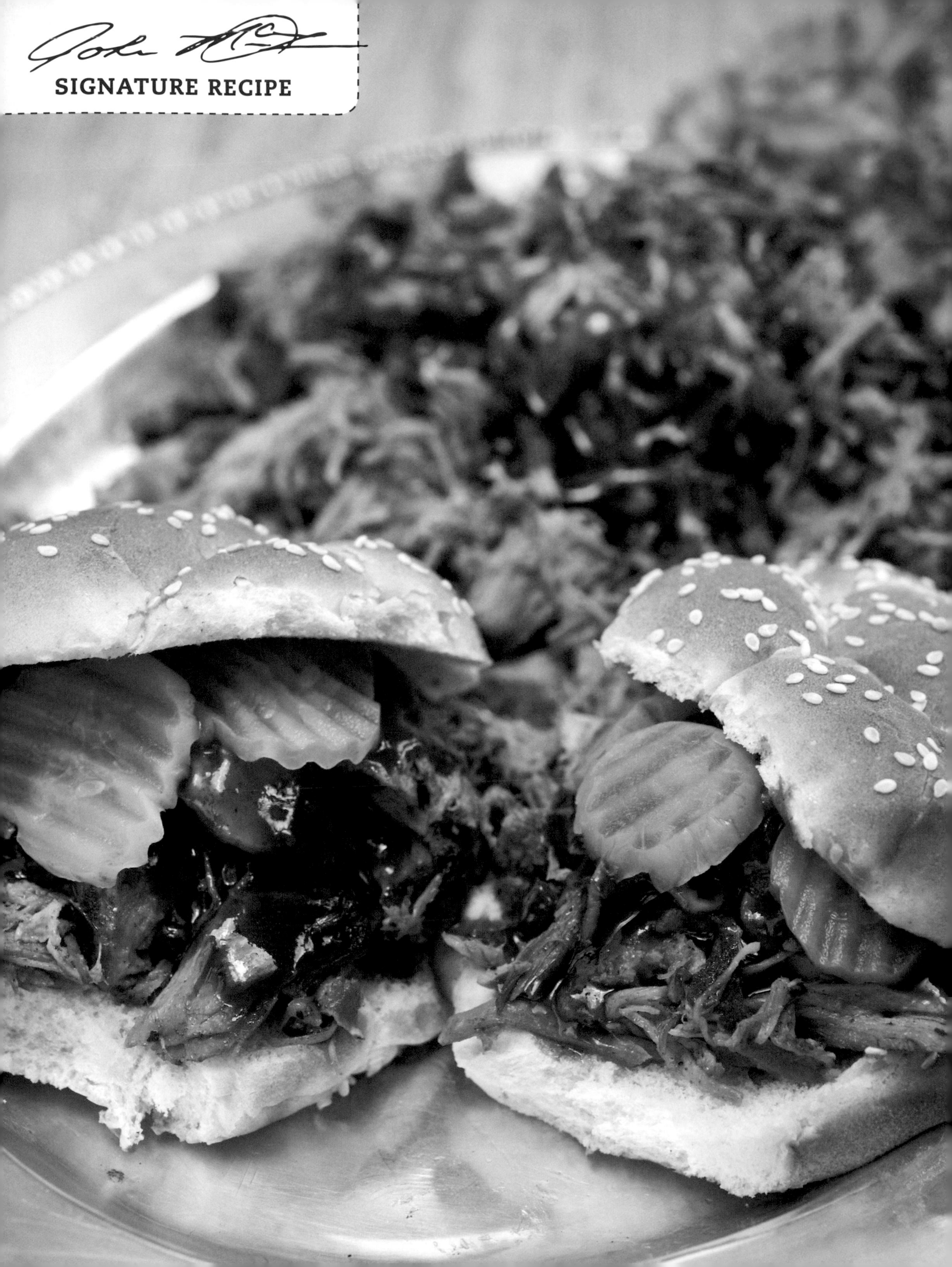

SIGNATURE RECIPE

PULLED PORK SANDWICHES
Serves 6 to 8

My brother Bill and niece Missy own Clearview BBQ in Columbus, GA. I tried and tried to get Missy to hand over their recipe for pulled pork sandwiches. She wouldn't surrender it, even for her favorite uncle! We developed this recipe for you, but if you're ever in Columbus, make sure you stop by Clearview and give their BBQ a try. (And ask Missy to give that recipe to her Uncle John!)

Instructions

1. Preheat smoker to 250°F.

2. Rinse meat and pat dry. In a small bowl, combine 3 tablespoons of the seasoning and onion salt. Rub dry mixture all over pork.

3. Cut 5 slits in top of pork butt and place a garlic clove in each. Place meat on middle rack of smoker and smoke for 2 1/2 hours. Remove meat and wrap in foil. Return to smoker and cook for an additional 2 1/2 hours or until internal temperature reaches 195°F.

You'll Need

- 1 pork butt (4 to 5 pounds)

- 5 tablespoons "DADGUM that's Good!"™ Seasoning (page 12), divided

- 1 tablespoon onion salt

- 5 cloves garlic

- 1 package large sandwich rolls

- 1 double recipe "DADGUM that's Good!"™ BBQ Sauce (page 13) or your favorite brand

- 1 (16-ounce) jar dill slices

▶ suggested wood
HICKORY

My brother and niece's BBQ place in Columbus, GA.

SMOKED SUGARY BACON WRAPS
Serves 8 to 10

I made these Smoked Sugary Bacon Wraps at my daughter Bailey's 14th birthday party. My intention was to serve them up as an appetizer for the adults, but the kids ate them up as soon as they were done! Some folks refer to these as "meat candy" because the brown sugar gives them a sweet flavor. Plan on making plenty of these because they disappear fast!

Instructions

1. Preheat smoker to 275°F.

2. Cut bacon strips into thirds lengthwise. Wrap each piece of bacon around a cocktail sausage. Pierce with a toothpick and dredge in brown sugar. Place on a baking sheet and then place on rack in smoker.

3. Smoke sausages for 2 to 2 1/2 hours, until bacon is crispy, making sure your baking sheet doesn't block the airflow along the sides of the smoker. You may also want to use a sheet that has holes for drainage. Another suggestion is to smoke them for about 15 minutes to absorb that delicious smokey flavor from the wood chips, then finish in the oven at 350°F for an additional 20 to 30 minutes, until bacon is cooked through.

You'll Need

- 1 (1-pound) package sliced bacon
- 1 (16-ounce) package cocktail sausages
- Toothpicks
- 1/2 cup packed brown sugar

❱ suggested wood
HICKORY

SMOKED CHERRY CHICKEN
Serves 2 to 4

Make sure you get the cherry marinade under the skin of these chicken quarters. This is a great way to infuse the flavors throughout. This chicken is juicy and flavorful when smoked, but you can also make this recipe on the grill (see Grilling Option, right). Using indirect heat, grill them for 45 minutes with the skin down and 30 minutes with the skin up. It is crucial to use indirect heat, since the cherry preserves have natural sugars that will burn over direct heat. Keep the grill on a medium setting. Make sure the chicken reaches an internal temperature of 165°F.

Instructions

1. Preheat smoker to 225°F.

2. In a medium bowl, combine cherry preserves, butter, lemon zest, lemon juice, cinnamon, salt and ground cloves. Brush marinade over chicken, reserving some marinade for basting during the cooking process.

3. Place chicken in smoker and smoke for 1 1/2 hours, basting halfway through or until internal temperature reaches 165°F.

You'll Need

- 1 cup cherry preserves

- 1 tablespoon butter or margarine, melted

- 1/2 teaspoon grated lemon zest

- 2 tablespoons fresh lemon juice

- 1 1/2 teaspoons ground cinnamon

- Pinch salt

- Pinch ground cloves

- 2 to 2 1/2 pounds chicken quarters

Grilling Option

Grill over indirect medium heat for 45 minutes with skin-side down, then 30 minutes with skin-side up.

▶ suggested wood
HICKORY

Lisa is my Assistant at Masterbuilt and her husband is Tim. We've come to think of them as family and have enjoyed time with them outside of work. One of the really cool things about Tim and Lisa is that they love to cook together. They enjoy using our Masterbuilt products to entertain their guests, and I've often wondered if they use our products more than we do! I love when they share their tips, recipes and techniques and love even more that they aren't afraid to try new things. They've even educated me on the brining process, which is used in this recipe. The lemon pepper flavor in this chicken is out of this world. Tim and Lisa aren't just dadgum good cooks, they are dadgum good friends!

Top: Tim, Lisa and me grilling.
Middle: Tim and Lisa in the kitchen.
Bottom: Tim and I cook up sweet potatoes to complement his chicken.

TIM AND LISA'S LEMON PEPPER CHICKEN

Serves 2 to 4

Instructions

1. Place 1/2 cup of the lemon pepper in a gallon-size resealable plastic bag or bowl. DO NOT add salt. Add 1 quart cold water and stir to mix. Rinse chicken and add to brine. Refrigerate for 2 hours or for up to 8 hours.

2. Preheat smoker to 225°F.

3. Remove chicken and pour out brine solution. Sprinkle remaining 2 teaspoons lemon pepper over the chicken. Don't be shy about this; the chicken can handle a liberal amount of seasoning.

4. Place chicken on middle rack of smoker, breast side up, and smoke for 4 hours (do not open the smoker during cooking) or until internal temperature reaches 165°F.

You'll Need

- 1/2 cup + 2 teaspoons lemon pepper

- 1 quart cold water

- 1 fresh or frozen whole chicken (3 1/2 pounds) or 2 Cornish game hens (each 1 1/2 pounds), thawed if frozen

▶ suggested wood
MESQUITE

SWEET 'N' SMOKEY GREEN BEANS
Serves 8 to 10

I like the challenge of taking a common, everyday dish and taking it up a notch. Green beans can be a bit boring, but adding brown sugar and bacon and smoking them takes them to a whole 'nutha level! When serving, you may want to sprinkle with additional brown sugar for an extra sweet dose of flavor.

Instructions

1. Preheat smoker to 250°F.

2. Drain beans and place in a 12-inch square disposable aluminum foil pan. Sprinkle garlic salt over beans. Cut butter in half and push the halves down into the beans.

3. Sprinkle brown sugar over beans and cover with bacon slices. (To be less sweet, cut back on sugar by 1/2 cup.) Cover with aluminum foil and place on the second rack of smoker and smoke for 1 1/2 hours. Remove aluminum foil and smoke for an additional 30 minutes. Remove from smoker and discard bacon. Stir beans well before serving.

You'll Need

- 2 cans (each 14 1/4-ounces) cut green beans, drained
- 1 tablespoon garlic salt
- 1 stick unsalted butter
- 2 cups packed light brown sugar
- 3 slices thick-cut bacon, halved

▶ suggested wood
HICKORY OR PECAN

ALOHA HAM

Serves 10 to 12

The marinade used for basting in this recipe adds a nice sweet flavor to your smoked ham. You can substitute teriyaki sauce for the soy sauce. In fact, if you have a bottle of teriyaki sauce on-hand, you can use it for another great recipe. Marinate fresh pineapple slices for about an hour in teriyaki sauce then grill over medium heat on the top rack for 2 to 3 minutes on each side. This grilled pineapple makes an awesome side dish for the Aloha Ham.

Instructions

1. Fill water tray 1/3 full with a 50/50 mixture of apple juice and water. Preheat smoker to 225°F.

2. In a small bowl, combine crushed pineapple, honey and soy sauce. Brush over ham, reserving enough to baste during the smoking process.

3. Attach pineapple slices to the ham with toothpicks. Place ham on bottom rack of smoker and smoke, basting every 2 hours with reserved marinade, for 4 to 6 hours or until internal temperature reaches 165°F (allow 30 to 45 minutes per pound).

You'll Need

- 50/50 mixture apple juice and water
- 1/4 cup crushed pineapple
- 1/4 cup honey
- 2 teaspoons soy sauce
- 1 precooked ham (10 pounds)
- 4 to 5 pineapple slices

▶ suggested wood
HICKORY

Masterbuilt's Marketing Director, Keith, has long bragged about his smoked beef brisket. Keith is a marketing whiz, but we had our doubts about whether he was a BBQ whiz. He won us over with this recipe. Leaving the fat-side up and following the steps to wrap at 150°F to 160°F internal temperature are keys to having a tender result in the end.

Top: *Keith, the Leprechaun, with Don and John.*
Middle: *Keith, Alex Rutledge (Bloodline), me and Don in the mountains.*
Bottom: *Fishing with Team Masterbuilt.*

KEITH'S BEEF BRISKET

Serves (1/2 pound of meat per person)

Instructions

1. Rub brisket with a layer of yellow mustard, then season liberally with your favorite steak seasoning and Cajun seasoning. Apply a layer of brown sugar. Use more or less brown sugar as needed to completely cover brisket. Wrap brisket or place in a container and marinate overnight in refrigerator.

2. Preheat smoker to 250°F.

3. Place brisket, fat side up, in smoker on middle rack and for a 6-pound brisket smoke for 2 to 3 hours or until internal temperature reaches 150°F to 160°F. (If using a 12-pound brisket, double your smoke time or smoke for 1 hour per pound for different size brisket.) When internal temperature of brisket reaches 150°F to 160°F, wrap brisket in aluminum foil or place in a disposable aluminum foil pan and cover with aluminum foil and smoke for another 2 to 3 hours or until internal temperature reaches 180°F to 190°F.

4. Remove brisket from smoker and let rest for 30 minutes before slicing. Slice meat perpendicular to grain.

You'll Need

- 6 to 12 pound beef brisket (that has at least a 1/4-inch of fat)

- 1/2 cup yellow mustard

- Steak seasoning

- Cajun seasoning

- 1 cup packed brown sugar

▶ **suggested wood**
HICKORY

SMOKEY SQUASH CASSEROLE
Serves 6 to 8

I love squash. In fact, one of my favorite ways to eat squash is when my wife, Tonya, pan-fries it on the stove top. When we were newlyweds, she cooked this squash over and over (and over and over....), because she knew how much I loved it. To this day, I'll never turn down her pan-fried squash, but I did want to offer up a new squash recipe in our house. Tonya was one of the key taste-testers during the development of this book. Not only did she love this recipe, she loved it again and again for leftovers for several days. As with other smoked veggie recipes in this book, follow the instructions carefully and be mindful not to oversmoke this dish. You want a hint of smokey flavor, without overpowering the casserole.

Instructions

1. Preheat smoker to 250°F.

2. In a large saucepan over medium-high heat, combine squash and onion, add water to cover and boil until tender. Drain and while still hot, add Velveeta cheese, Alouette cheeses, mayonnaise, parsley flakes, hot sauce, Cajun seasoning, salt, and pepper. Stir until cheeses melt. Add eggs and mix well.

3. Crush crackers and place in a medium bowl. In a small saucepan, melt butter. Pour over crackers, mixing well. Add 1/2 cup to the squash mixture, mixing well. Pour into 8-inch square disposable aluminum foil pan. Sprinkle remaining crackers over squash. Cover with aluminum foil.

4. Place on lower rack of smoker and smoke for 1 hour. Add one small handful of wood chips to smoker, then remove foil from squash casserole. Smoke casserole for 10 to 15 minutes. Remove from smoker and serve.

You'll Need

- 2 1/2 pounds yellow squash, sliced
- 1 medium yellow onion, chopped
- 1 (3-ounce) package Velveeta cheese
- 1/2 cup Alouette Sun-Dried and Basil cheese spread or your favorite variety
- 1/4 cup Alouette Garlic and Herb cheese spread or your favorite variety
- 1/4 cup mayonnaise
- 2 tablespoons dried parsley flakes
- 3/4 teaspoon hot sauce (your favorite variety)
- 1/4 teaspoon Cajun seasoning
- 1/4 teaspoon salt
- 1/4 teaspoon freshly ground black pepper
- 2 eggs, beaten
- 1 sleeve saltine crackers, crushed
- 1/2 cup butter

▶ suggested wood
HICKORY

SMOKIN' HOT STUFFED PORK CHOPS
Serves 6

Some may say it's a bit overboard to stuff pork chops with pork sausage, but I would not be included in that "some." I love the flavor of the sausage stuffing in these chops. To save time and effort, you can ask your butcher to go ahead and cut the pockets in these chops for you.

Instructions

1. Preheat smoker to 250°F.

2. Cook rice according to package directions.

3. Meanwhile, in a skillet over medium heat, brown pork sausage. Drain and set aside. Cut a pocket in each chop by making a horizontal cut through the meat almost to the bone.

4. In a medium bowl, combine cooked rice, pork sausage and 1/4 teaspoon of the Cajun seasoning. Spoon stuffing loosely into pockets. Sprinkle with remaining 1/4 teaspoon of Cajun seasoning and black pepper.

5. Place pork chops on middle rack of smoker and smoke for 1 hour to 1 hour and 15 minutes or until the internal temperature reaches 160°F.

You'll Need

- 1 cup uncooked rice (your favorite type)

- 1 pound hot or mild pork sausage

- 6 pork chops, center cut (each 3/4- to 1-inch thick)

- 1/2 teaspoon Cajun seasoning, divided

- 1/2 teaspoon freshly ground black pepper

▶ suggested wood
APPLE

Top: *One of the greatest sportsmen I know and my dadgum good friend, Bill Jordan of Realtree.*

Middle: *After a hunt with J-Mac and Brooke.*

Bottom: *Huntin' with J-Mac.*

SPORTSMAN'S JERKY
Serves 8 to 12

I live in an area of the South where hunting of all types is very popular. Sportsmen love jerky and this recipe works well with beef or venison. Keith from Masterbuilt loves to hunt and fish and shared this recipe with us. Whether you're a sportsman or not, this is a great homemade snack to keep in your pantry.

Instructions

1. Cut meat into thin slices, about 1/8 inch thick. The butcher where you purchase the meat may cut the meat for you. Ask him to cut it into 1/8 inch thick slices (or as thin as he can get it). If you end up cutting the meat yourself, place in the freezer until firm but not frozen. Remove meat from freezer and then slice.

2. **Marinade:** In a large bowl, combine teriyaki marinade and hot and spicy marinade. Place meat in bowl and refrigerate for 6 hours to overnight. If you can't find the Allegro hot and spicy marinade use 1 cup of Dale's (or Moore's) marinade and 1 teaspoon crushed red peppers. You can increase the amounts of marinades in a 1 to 1 ratio if more is required to completely cover meat. You can also experiment with the ratio of marinades using more or less hot and spicy marinade to suit your taste.

3. When replacing beef with venison, soak venison in cold water with 1 tablespoon salt until water is bloody. Pour off water and repeat this process a second time. Make sure venison has been in the freezer for at least 6 months before making jerky and all the meat membrane and fat has been trimmed.

4. Preheat smoker to 250°F.

5. Place meat onto the racks in smoker, making sure not to overlap meat pieces. Make sure the air vent on your smoker is completely open when making jerky. Smoke for 6 to 9 hours or until meat is dried completely and hard to the touch. Jerky should bend but not break.

You'll Need

- 1 beef round roast or round steak (2 to 3 pounds), trimmed of fat

- 2 to 3 lbs of hind quarter roast with fat and membrane trimmed (optional)

Marinade

- 1 cup Allegro Teriyaki Marinade or your favorite brand

- 1 cup Allegro Hot & Spicy Marinade or your favorite brand

Oven Option

Line the lowest oven rack with aluminum foil to catch dripping and preheat oven to 200 degrees. Place jerky on higher racks and bake for 6 to 9 hours or until meat is dried completely and hard to the touch. Jerky should bend but not break.

▶ suggested wood
HICKORY

Georgia is the "Peach State." And as a good ol' Georgia boy, I love anything with peaches. Peach cobbler, peach pie, peach smoothies, peach jam....and I'm even married to a Georgia Peach! You may not think of peaches when you think of smoked Cornish hens, but trust me, they are dadgum good. If you've got a hungry crowd, plan on one hen per guest, but you can split them in half and feed two adults per hen.

GEORGIA PEACH HENS

Serves 2

Instructions

1. Preheat smoker to 225°F.

2. In a bowl, combine peach preserves, orange juice, cinnamon, salt and ginger to create a glaze. Brush glaze over Cornish game hens. Place hens on middle rack of smoker and smoke hens for 3 1/2 hours or until internal temperature reaches 165°F.

You'll Need

- 1/3 cup peach preserves
- 1 tablespoon orange juice
- 1/4 teaspoon ground cinnamon
- Pinch salt
- Pinch ground ginger
- 2 Cornish game hens, rinsed thoroughly and patted dry (each 1 1/2 pounds)

▶ suggested wood
APPLE

- 1/4 cup Heinz 57 Sauce
- 1/4 cup A1 Steak Sauce
- 2 tablespoons extra virgin olive oil
- 2 tablespoons red wine vinegar
- 2 tablespoons Worcestershire sauce
- 1 tablespoon onion powder
- 2 teaspoons minced garlic
- Garlic salt
- Freshly ground black pepper
- 6 beef filet steaks (each 1-inch thick)

SMOKED BEEF FILET STEAKS
Serves 6

Nothing compares to an awesome grilled steak and we've got some dadgum good grilled steak recipes in this book. If you've got some extra time, I'd highly recommend giving smoked steaks a try. You won't have to babysit them over the grill and won't even have to turn them during the cooking process. They have a smoke-infused flavor and juicy result.

Doneness Chart

125°F Rare

135°F Medium-Rare

145°F Medium

155°F Medium-Well

165°F Well Done

Instructions

1. In a medium bowl, combine Heinz 57 Sauce, A1 Steak Sauce, olive oil, red wine vinegar, Worcestershire sauce, onion powder, minced garlic, garlic salt, and pepper to taste, mixing well. Place steaks in a resealable plastic bag. Pour marinade over steaks, seal and refrigerate. Marinate, turning occasionally, for at least 4 hours or overnight.

2. Preheat smoker to 225°F.

3. Place steaks on lower rack of smoker and smoke for 35 to 40 minutes or until internal temperature reaches desired doneness (see Doneness Chart to the right).

▶ suggested wood
HICKORY

You'll Need

- 50/50 mixture apple juice and water
- 3/4 cup red wine vinegar
- 3/4 cup soy sauce
- 3/4 cup honey
- 2 tablespoons garlic salt
- 2 tablespoons freshly ground black pepper
- 1 whole duck (5 to 6 pounds)

SMOKED DUCK
Serves 6 to 8

Make sure you carefully monitor the internal temperature of the duck so you don't dry out the breast. It's great served alone, but I'd also suggest making a smoked duck club sandwich. Slice the duck and serve on toasted bread with lettuce, tomato, smoked bacon slices and the dipping sauce from our Fried Cauliflower recipe on page 127.

Instructions

1. Preheat smoker to 250°F. Add 50/50 mixture of apple juice and water to water tray.

2. In a medium bowl, combine red wine vinegar, soy sauce, honey, garlic salt and pepper. Place duck in a gallon-size resealable plastic bag. Reserve 1/2 cup marinade for later use. Pour remaining marinade over duck. Refrigerate and marinate for 2 to 4 hours.

3. Place duck on middle rack of smoker and smoke, uncovered, for 1 hour, basting several times with reserved marinade. When well browned, cover with aluminum foil and smoke for 2 1/2 to 4 hours or until internal temperature reaches 165°F.

▶ suggested wood
APPLE

I've spent a lot of time at QVC over the past 10 years and developed relationships with chefs and food stylists on the sets. Nick is our food stylist, friend and all-around-great-guy. When we come in to town for an airing, he knows we always want a tray and foil to wrap up our favorite dish — prime rib! He smokes a lot of food for us at the Q, and it's all dadgum good, but nothing holds a candle to his prime rib. We bring it home to our family in Georgia and feast on the leftovers for several nights. In fact, I'll let you in on a little secret — slice up the leftover prime rib and sear on the grill. Don't overcook it — sear it just long enough to get it warm. If you've ever watched our segments on QVC and drooled over the prime rib, now it's your turn to recreate the drool-effect in your own backyard!

Top: *Cutting up at QVC with Nick and Mitch, our food stylists.*

Bottom: *Thumbs up from John and Nick.*

You'll Need

- 4 cloves garlic, chopped

- 2 tablespoons kosher salt

- 1 tablespoon freshly ground black pepper

- 1 tablespoon dried thyme

- 1 prime rib roast, boned (4 to 6 pounds)

Doneness Chart

125°F Rare

135°F Medium-Rare

145°F Medium

155°F Medium-Well

165°F Well Done

I don't recommend Well Done for a prime rib.

NICK'S PRIME RIB
Serves 6 to 8

Instructions

1. Preheat smoker to 250°F.

2. In a small bowl, combine garlic, salt, pepper and thyme. Coat prime rib evenly with seasoning. Place roast, fat side up, directly on middle rack in smoker. Reduce temperature to 225°F, smoke roast for 4 to 6 hours for medium-rare to medium (1 hour per pound) or until desired temperature (see Doneness Chart to the right) (Remember, meat will continue to cook for a few minutes when taken out of the smoker and covered with aluminum foil.)

3. Once you have removed the prime rib, cover it with aluminum foil and let rest for 15 to 20 minutes before cutting. This will help keep the prime rib warm and juicy.

❯ suggested wood
HICKORY OR APPLE

SMOKED TURKEY BREAST
Serves 8 to 10

We eat a lot of turkey at the McLemore house and I'm always puzzled at folks who only eat turkey at the holidays. If you're intimidated about smoking a whole turkey, don't be. We have a couple of great whole turkey recipes in this book. Another way to enjoy turkey year-round is to cook a turkey breast. You can slice it for sandwiches, serve on a dinner plate with veggies, or chop and make a turkey salad. Smoking this injected turkey breast keeps it from drying out and gives you a moist, tender result every time.

Instructions

1. Preheat smoker to 225°F.

2. Wash turkey well and pat dry. Using a marinade injection syringe, inject turkey breast with 6 to 7 ounces Creole Injection Marinade, one ounce at a time, in several locations over breast. Rub "DADGUM That's Good!"™ Seasoning over turkey.

3. Place on middle rack of smoker and smoke for 4 1/2 to 5 hours, about 45 minutes per pound, or until internal temperature reaches 165°F.

You'll Need

- 1 turkey breast (6 to 7 pounds)

- (6 to 7 ounces) Butterball Buttery Creole Injection Marinade

- 1 recipe "DADGUM That's Good!"™ Seasoning (page 12)

▶ suggested wood
HICKORY

You'll Need

- 2 fresh or frozen whole chickens (each 3 1/2 pounds), thawed if frozen

- 2 tablespoons extra virgin olive oil

- 3 tablespoons seasoned salt

- 1 tablespoon cracked black peppercorns

- 2 teaspoons ground sage

- 1 teaspoon Jane's Krazy Mixed-Up Salt

SMOKED WHOLE CHICKENS
Serves 6 to 8

One of the challenges we face when smoking whole turkeys or chickens is that the cooking time may vary due to the size of the bird and the water content in the poultry. Marinades, injections and brines can affect the cooking time for a recipe. The key to smoking the perfect chicken is carefully monitoring the internal temperature. I highly recommend using a digital meat probe thermometer. When the internal temperature of the meat reaches 165°F, it's ready!

Instructions

1.   Preheat smoker to 250°F.

2.   Rinse chickens and pat dry. Brush 1 tablespoon of the olive oil on each chicken. In a small bowl, combine seasoned salt, cracked black peppercorns, sage and Krazy salt. Sprinkle mixture over each chicken. Tie legs and wings together with cooking twine. Place chickens on the middle rack of smoker and smoke for 2 to 5 hours or until internal temperature reaches 165°F. Check internal temperature at the 2-hour mark.

▶ suggested wood
HICKORY

MEMAW'S SOUTHERN FRIED CHICKEN

Serves 4 to 6

Truth be told, we had another fried chicken recipe for this cookbook. It was a spicy recipe that tasted good, but as with any other fried chicken I try, it paled in comparison to my Momma's fried chicken. Momma (also known as MeMaw) passed away in December of 2011, and I dedicated this book to her. I can't imagine printing any other fried chicken recipe in this book, so her recipe makes an encore appearance. Serve it up with some mashed potatoes and biscuits for the ultimate Southern comfort meal. It's nice to have recipes like this to keep MeMaw's memory going strong around our kitchen table.

Instructions

1. Fill deep fryer halfway with oil and heat to 375°F.

2. Sprinkle chicken with salt and pepper. Pour buttermilk into a medium bowl. Place the flour in another medium bowl. Dip chicken pieces in buttermilk, coating them well, then dredge in flour.

3. Place chicken pieces in the fryer and cook for 15 minutes until golden brown. Use a metal slotted spoon to transfer to paper towels to drain.

You'll Need

- 1 gallon cooking oil
- 1 fryer chicken (3 pounds), cut into pieces
- 1 teaspoon salt
- 1 teaspoon black pepper
- 1 cup buttermilk
- 1 cup self-rising flour

Momma with Daddy on his 73rd birthday.

GARLIC AND HERB DEEP-FRIED TURKEY

Serves 6 to 12

One of the signature dishes in my first cookbook was the Cajun Deep-Fried Turkey and Buffalo Sauce. That Cajun turkey remains one of my favorite recipes, but this garlic and herb version runs a close second. Frying a turkey in hot oil calls for a cool head and a fair measure of caution. You want to start with a turkey that's fully thawed and dry; oil and water do not mix! Without doubt, the best and safest way to fry a turkey is with Masterbuilt's Butterball® Indoor Electric Turkey Fryer. With no propane and no flame, you can have peace of mind and a dadgum good fried turkey! In fact, our deep-fried turkeys are so dadgum good, the McLemores serve up at least two of them every holiday.

You'll Need

- 1 fresh or frozen whole turkey (10 to 14 pounds)

- 2 gallons cooking oil, preferably peanut oil

- 1 (16-ounce) bottle Butterball Garlic and Herb Turkey Marinade or your favorite brand

- Butterball Garlic and Herb Turkey Seasoning or your favorite brand

Instructions

1. Thaw turkey, if frozen. To properly thaw a frozen turkey in the refrigerator allow approximately 24 hours for every 4 pounds. Fill deep fryer halfway with oil and heat to 375°F. Remove giblets and neck. If present, remove and discard plastic leg holder and pop-up timer. Rinse turkey thoroughly with warm water or completely cover with warm water and soak for no more than 30 minutes to ensure cavity is free of ice.

2. Pat turkey completely dry on outside and inside of cavity with paper towels. Using a marinade injection syringe, inject 1/2 cup (4 ounces) marinade in each breast. Inject 1/4 cup (2 ounces) marinade into each leg and thigh. Sprinkle turkey generously with turkey seasoning, completely coating the outside of the turkey and inside of the cavity.

3. Place turkey, breast side up, in fryer basket. Slowly lower the basket into hot oil, being careful not to splatter hot oil. Fry turkey for 3 to 4 minutes per pound. Lift the basket from the hot oil slowly. Insert a meat thermometer in the meaty part of the breast; turkey is done when it reads 165°F. If the turkey is not done, lower it carefully back into the oil for an additional 5 minutes. Once the turkey reaches the desired temperature (minimum 165°F), remove from oil.

4. Allow the turkey to rest and drain in the fryer basket for 10 minutes before removing for carving. The turkey can remain in the basket to cool until ready to serve.

Bailey and me (2 turkeys), frying a turkey on tour in New York at Fox. A DADGUM Good day for me.

BUTTERMILK-BATTERED ONION RINGS

Serves 4 to 6

When frying onion rings, make sure you don't stack them in the oil. Fry them in small batches so they won't clump together. The thickness of your onion slices will affect your frying time. As an option, you can also make onion "petals" by slicing the rings in half before you batter and fry.

Instructions

1. Fill deep fryer halfway with oil and heat to 350°F.

2. Cut onions in 1/4-inch thick slices and separate into rings.

3. In a large shallow dish, whisk together flour and baking powder. In another large bowl, combine buttermilk and eggs, mixing well. Dip onion rings in buttermilk mixture, then dredge in flour mixture.

4. Fry onion rings in batches, turning once, for 2 to 3 minutes or until golden. Use a metal slotted spoon to transfer to paper towels to drain. Sprinkle with salt to taste and serve immediately.

You'll Need

- 1 gallon cooking oil
- 2 large sweet onions
- 1 cup all-purpose flour
- 1/2 teaspoon baking powder
- 1 cup buttermilk
- 2 eggs, lightly beaten
- Salt

FRIED CORN WITH LIME BUTTER
Serves 4

You'll Need

- 1 gallon cooking oil
- 1 tablespoon butter
- 2 tablespoons fresh lime juice
- 1/2 cup all-purpose flour
- 1/2 teaspoon baking powder
- 1/4 teaspoon kosher salt
- 1/2 cup club soda
- 2 ears corn, halved

When I was a kid, I remember going with my Dad to pick up fresh corn and loading the back of his truck to the brim. The kids would shuck the corn together and Dad would cook the corn one of three ways: boiled, boiled or boiled. Thankfully, we've learned several other ways to cook corn since those days! I love the taste of fried corn on the cob. You can deep-fry the fresh cob or try this method of dipping in batter and frying. Either way, the lime butter makes a dadgum good complement to the corn.

Instructions

1. Fill deep fryer halfway with oil and heat to 350°F.

2. In a small saucepan, melt butter over medium-low heat. Add lime juice, stirring well. Keep warm.

3. In a large bowl, combine flour, baking powder and salt. Stir in club soda, mixing well. Dip corn in flour mixture and fry in batches, turning once, for 6 to 7 minutes or until golden. Use a metal slotted spoon to transfer to paper towels to drain. Pour lime butter over corn and serve immediately.

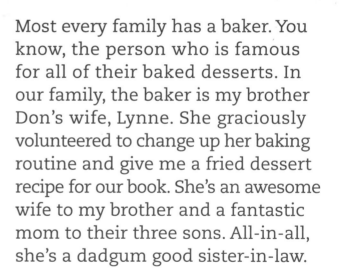

Most every family has a baker. You know, the person who is famous for all of their baked desserts. In our family, the baker is my brother Don's wife, Lynne. She graciously volunteered to change up her baking routine and give me a fried dessert recipe for our book. She's an awesome wife to my brother and a fantastic mom to their three sons. All-in-all, she's a dadgum good sister-in-law.

Top: Our families in Gulf Shores — Grillin' for the Gulf and makin' memories.
Right: Lynne, MeMaw and Tonya
Left: Lynne and Don at the Sound Choices Gala.
Bottom: Lynne and Tonya show off the Butterball® Indoor Electric Turkey Fryer.

LYNNE'S APPLE FRITTERS

Makes 12

Instructions

1. Fill deep fryer halfway with oil and heat to 350°F.

2. In a large bowl, combine flour, apples, granulated sugar, baking powder, cinnamon and salt. Stir in egg and milk.

3. Drop batter by tablespoonfuls into hot oil and fry in batches, turning once, for 7 to 8 minutes or until golden brown. Use a metal slotted spoon to transfer to paper towels to drain. Serve immediately with confectioners' sugar, honey and/or cinnamon sugar.

You'll Need

- 1 gallon cooking oil

- 1 cup all-purpose flour

- 1 3/4 cups diced apples

- 2 tablespoons granulated sugar

- 1 teaspoon baking powder

- 1/2 teaspoon ground cinnamon

- 1/2 teaspoon salt

- 1 egg, lightly beaten

- 1/2 cup milk

- Confectioners' sugar

- Honey

- 2 tablespoons cinnamon sugar (a combination of equal amounts ground cinnamon and granulated sugar)

EGGPLANT FRIES
Serves 8 to 10

My momma made fried eggplant when we were kids and would invite us into the kitchen to help out. We cut the eggplant into spears and sliced those into smaller, triangular-shaped chunks. We had fun breading them together before she fried them. Cut them any way you choose, but I'll always prefer my momma's way! Any way you slice them, they are dadgum good. I'd highly recommend pairing them with the Chipotle Dipping Sauce on page 121.

Instructions

1. Place eggplant in a large bowl. Add 2 cups ice and enough water to cover. Cover and refrigerate until chilled, for at least 1 hour.

2. Fill deep fryer halfway with oil and heat to 350°F.

3. In a large bowl, combine cornmeal, garlic powder and salt. Drain eggplant and dip in cornmeal mixture to coat. Fry eggplant in batches for 3 minutes or until golden brown. Use a metal slotted spoon to transfer to paper towels to drain. Serve immediately.

You'll Need

- 1 pound eggplant, cut crosswise into 1/2-inch strips

- 1 gallon cooking oil

- 2 cups white cornmeal

- 1 tablespoon garlic powder

- 1/2 teaspoon kosher salt

Any time with Momma was always time well spent. She was such a great cook.

FRIED MUSHROOMS WITH KICKIN' RANCH SAUCE

Serves 8

Here's another recipe that you would see on the appetizer portion of the menu at your favorite restaurant. Enjoying fried mushrooms at home with family and friends is even better than fighting the crowds and dining out. You can leave out the cayenne pepper in the dipping sauce if you have a more sensitive palate, but I like to double the cayenne!

Instructions

1. Fill deep fryer halfway with oil and heat to 350°F.

2. In a large shallow dish, combine panko, parsley, lemon zest, salt and pepper, mixing well. In another large shallow dish, combine eggs and buttermilk. Dip mushrooms in buttermilk and then dredge in bread crumb mixture. Place on a large baking sheet.

3. **Kickin' Ranch Sauce:** In a small bowl, combine Ranch dressing, bacon and cayenne, stirring well. Cover and refrigerate until ready to serve or for up to 2 days.

4. Fry mushrooms in batches, turning once at 90 seconds, for 2 1/2 to 3 minutes or until golden brown. Use a metal slotted spoon to transfer to paper towels to drain. Serve immediately with Kickin' Ranch Sauce.

You'll Need

- 1 gallon cooking oil
- 2 cups panko bread crumbs
- 2 tablespoons dried parsley flakes
- 2 teaspoons grated lemon zest
- 1/2 teaspoon kosher salt
- 1/2 teaspoon freshly ground black pepper
- 4 eggs, lightly beaten
- 1 cup buttermilk
- 1 pound whole button mushrooms

Kickin' Ranch Sauce

- 1 cup Ranch salad dressing
- 3 slices cooked bacon, crumbled
- 1/4 teaspoon cayenne pepper

You'll Need

- 1 gallon cooking oil
- 1 large egg, lightly beaten
- 1 cup club soda
- 1 3/4 cups all-purpose flour
- 1 teaspoon baking powder
- 1 (16-ounce) jar dill pickle sandwich slices, drained

Ranch Dipping Sauce

- 1/4 cup Ranch salad dressing
- 2 tablespoons salsa

FRIED PICKLES WITH RANCH DIPPING SAUCE

Serves 8

A staple item on the menu at Southern fish camp restaurants is fried pickles. You will find them in the "hamburger-chip" small-slice version or in a longer sandwich-slice version. You don't have to wait on a trip to the restaurant to enjoy this flavorful indulgence. I prefer the sandwich slices and love to dip them in ranch dressing. For an extra kick of flavor, choose a spicy ranch or bacon ranch dressing.

Instructions

1. Fill deep fryer halfway with oil and heat to 350°F.

2. In a shallow dish, whisk together egg and club soda. In another shallow dish or medium bowl, combine flour and baking powder. Dip pickle slices in egg mixture and then dredge in flour mixture.

3. **Ranch Dipping Sauce:** In a small bowl, combine ranch dressing and salsa, mixing well. Cover and refrigerate until ready to serve or for up to 1 day.

4. Fry pickles in batches, turning once, for 2 to 2 1/2 minutes or until golden. Use a metal slotted spoon to transfer to paper towels to drain. Serve immediately with Ranch Dipping Sauce.

CRABMEAT BALLS
Serves 8 to 10

When selecting the ingredients for this recipe, finding fresh crabmeat is best, but it's not always available. Substituting ready-to-serve crabmeat is the next best thing. Just remember — add an additional 2 minutes to the cooking time if using fresh/raw crabmeat.

Instructions

1.   In a large bowl, combine bread crumbs, butter, parsley, Dijon mustard, Old Bay seasoning and salt. Add crabmeat and eggs, mixing well. Cover and chill in the refrigerator for at least 1 hour.

2.   Fill deep fryer halfway with oil and heat to 350°F.

3.   Place flour in a shallow bowl. Shape crabmeat mixture into 1-inch balls and dredge in flour.

4.   Fry crabmeat balls in batches, turning once, for 2 to 3 minutes or until golden. Use a metal slotted spoon to transfer to paper towels to drain. Serve immediately with cocktail or tartar sauce.

You'll Need

- 1/2 cup plain bread crumbs
- 1/4 cup butter, melted
- 2 tablespoons chopped fresh Italian parsley
- 1 tablespoon Dijon mustard
- 3/4 to 1 teaspoon Old Bay seasoning
- 1/4 teaspoon sea salt
- 1 pound ready-to-serve lump crabmeat, drained
- 2 eggs, lightly beaten
- 1 gallon cooking oil
- 1/2 cup all-purpose flour
- Cocktail or tartar sauce

My daughter Bailey loves chicken fingers. She loves them even more when hosting a sleepover with a ton of her friends! This recipe freezes well once breaded, so we can make them in advance and stock the freezer. This way we have plenty on-hand for last-minute parties. Be sure to add 1 to 2 minutes to the frying time if the chicken fingers are frozen. Any recipe that I can make with my kids is dadgum good!

Top: One of many slumber parties at our house. Wall to wall girls for Bailey's 9th birthday.
Middle: Bailey is the baby of the family. She was a cute two-year old, wasn't she?
Left: Bailey is growing into a beautiful young lady.

BAILEY'S CHICKEN FINGERS WITH HONEY MUSTARD

Serves 4

Instructions

1. Fill deep fryer halfway with oil and heat to 350°F.

2. In a small bowl, combine Dijon mustard and honey, stirring well. Set aside.

3. In a medium shallow dish, combine egg and buttermilk. In another bowl, combine crackers, bread crumbs and pepper. Dip chicken in egg mixture and then dredge in bread crumb mixture.

4. Fry chicken in batches, turning as needed, for 3 to 4 minutes or until golden brown. Use a metal slotted spoon to transfer to paper towels to drain. Serve immediately with honey mustard mixture.

You'll Need

- 1 gallon cooking oil

- 1/2 cup Dijon mustard

- 6 tablespoons honey

- 1 egg, lightly beaten

- 1/2 cup buttermilk

- 1 cup crushed crackers (about 20), such as saltines

- 1 cup seasoned bread crumbs

- 1/2 teaspoon freshly ground black pepper

- 1 1/4 pounds chicken tenders

FRIED PIMENTO CHEESE BALLS
Makes 12

Another Southern staple is pimento cheese. You'd be hard pressed to find someone in the South who wasn't raised on pimento cheese sandwiches. As much as I love pimento cheese on white bread or crackers, I've found my new favorite way to enjoy it — deep-fried! Make sure you don't chill the balls in the freezer for longer than an 1 1/2 hours; you don't want them to hard-freeze. You should also give Christy's Smoked Pimento Cheese Appetizer a try (page 57). In fact, use that leftover pimento cheese dip to make this recipe. That's like having your cake — I mean, pimento cheese — and eating it, too!

You'll Need

- 1 (12-ounce) container pimento cheese spread
- 1 gallon cooking oil
- 1 1/2 cups all-purpose flour
- 1/2 teaspoon cayenne pepper
- 2 eggs, lightly beaten
- 1 1/2 cups panko bread crumbs

Instructions

1. Using a teaspoon, form pimento cheese into 1-inch balls and place onto wax paper. Freeze for 1 hour to stiffen the balls to allow you to shape before breading.

2. Fill deep fryer halfway with oil and heat to 375°F.

3. Set up three bowls for breading. In the first bowl, combine flour and cayenne. Place beaten eggs in the second bowl. Place panko in the third bowl. Dredge the pimento cheese balls in flour, then egg, then roll in panko. Place balls on a baking sheet and refrigerate for 20 minutes.

4. Fry balls a few at a time for 2 to 3 minutes or until golden brown. Use a metal slotted spoon to transfer to paper towels to drain.

FRIED SOFT-SHELL CRABS
Serves 6

The beauty of soft-shell crabs is that you can eat them whole — no need to crack them and dig for the meat! These fried soft-shell crabs can be served alone or on bread with sliced tomatoes. The Rémoulade Sauce from our Smoked Shrimp Po' Boys with Rémoulade Sauce on page 58 makes a nice complement.

You'll Need

- 1 gallon cooking oil
- 1 cup milk
- 2 large eggs, lightly beaten
- 6 soft-shell crabs
- 1 teaspoon sea salt
- 1/2 teaspoon freshly ground black pepper
- 1 1/2 cups self-rising flour
- Toppings (optional)
  Lemons
  Cocktail sauce
  Tartar sauce
- Parsley (optional)

Instructions

1. Fill deep fryer halfway with oil and heat to 350°F.

2. In a medium bowl, whisk together milk and eggs. Set aside.

3. Rinse crabs and pat dry. Sprinkle with salt and pepper. Place flour in a shallow bowl. Dredge crabs in flour, dip in milk mixture and dredge in flour again.

4. Fry in batches for 2 minutes on each side or until golden brown. Use a metal slotted spoon to transfer to paper towels to drain. Serve immediately with lemons, cocktail sauce or tartar sauce, if using. Garnish with parsley, if using.

FRIED SCALLOPS IN BACON

Serves 8 to 10

When I was about 12 years old, my dad took us to Port St. Joe, Florida, to go scalloping. We would catch the scallops and cook them up for dinner. Wrapping them in bacon always gave them great flavor. After our bellies were full, we'd spend the night at the beach campground in the back of our dad's truck camper. This camper built for two slept seven McLemores!

Instructions

1. Fill deep fryer halfway with oil and heat to 350°F.

2. In a small bowl, combine flour, 1/2 teaspoon of salt and 1/2 teaspoon of pepper. Set aside.

3. In another bowl, combine scallops, lemon zest, lemon juice and remaining 1/4 teaspoon each of salt and pepper. Let stand for 15 minutes.

4. Toss scallops in flour mixture, coating well. Wrap 1 bacon slice around each scallop, double wrapping the bacon and securing tightly with a toothpick.

5. Fry scallops in batches for 2 to 3 minutes or until golden brown. Use a metal slotted spoon to transfer to paper towels to drain. Serve immediately.

You'll Need

- 1 gallon cooking oil

- 3/4 cup all-purpose flour

- 3/4 teaspoon sea salt, divided

- 3/4 teaspoon freshly ground black pepper, divided

- 1/2 pound sea scallops (about 12)

- 1 teaspoon grated lemon zest

- 1 tablespoon fresh lemon juice

- 12 slices bacon

- Toothpicks

This was not our dad's camper, but Don and I did some camping in my truck camper with Tonya and Lynne. The beginning of great memories.

My wife's mother, Shirley, has always been known for keeping a meticulously neat and clean home. In fact, we would probably use the term Shirley-homemaker instead of Susie-homemaker! Tonya and her brother Chris loved Shirley's fried salmon patties when they were little. Shirley didn't like the smell of that salmon, and really didn't like handling it in her clean kitchen, but she made the sacrifice and cooked up those salmon patties regularly for the kids. That's one of the things I respect and admire about Shirley, and my wife for that matter. They know what their kids love and don't let something like a smelly ol' fish keep them from delivering the goods!

Top: *My brother-in-law Chris, Shirley and Tonya.*

Bottom: *Early years in the kitchen. I'm carving a deep-fried turkey and Tonya is helping Shirley.*

SHIRLEY'S SALMON PATTIES
Serves 6

Instructions

1. Fill deep fryer halfway with oil and heat to 350°F.

2. Remove skin from salmon and chop in a food processor or with a knife; do not overprocess. In a large bowl, combine salmon, onion, eggs, Cajun seasoning, cracked peppercorns and Greek dressing.

3. Using a 1/3 cup measure for each patty, shape mixture into 6 patties and roll each in crushed crackers.

4. Place in fryer, turning once, and fry for 2 1/2 to 3 minutes or until patties are golden brown and float to the top. Use a metal slotted spoon to transfer to paper towels to drain. Serve with your favorite sauce.

You'll Need

- 1 gallon cooking oil
- 2 pounds fresh salmon
- 3/4 cup chopped yellow onion
- 2 eggs, well beaten
- 2 teaspoons Cajun seasoning
- 1/8 teaspoon cracked black peppercorns
- 1/3 cup Ken's Steakhouse Greek Dressing
- 1 sleeve saltine crackers, crushed

SIGNATURE RECIPE

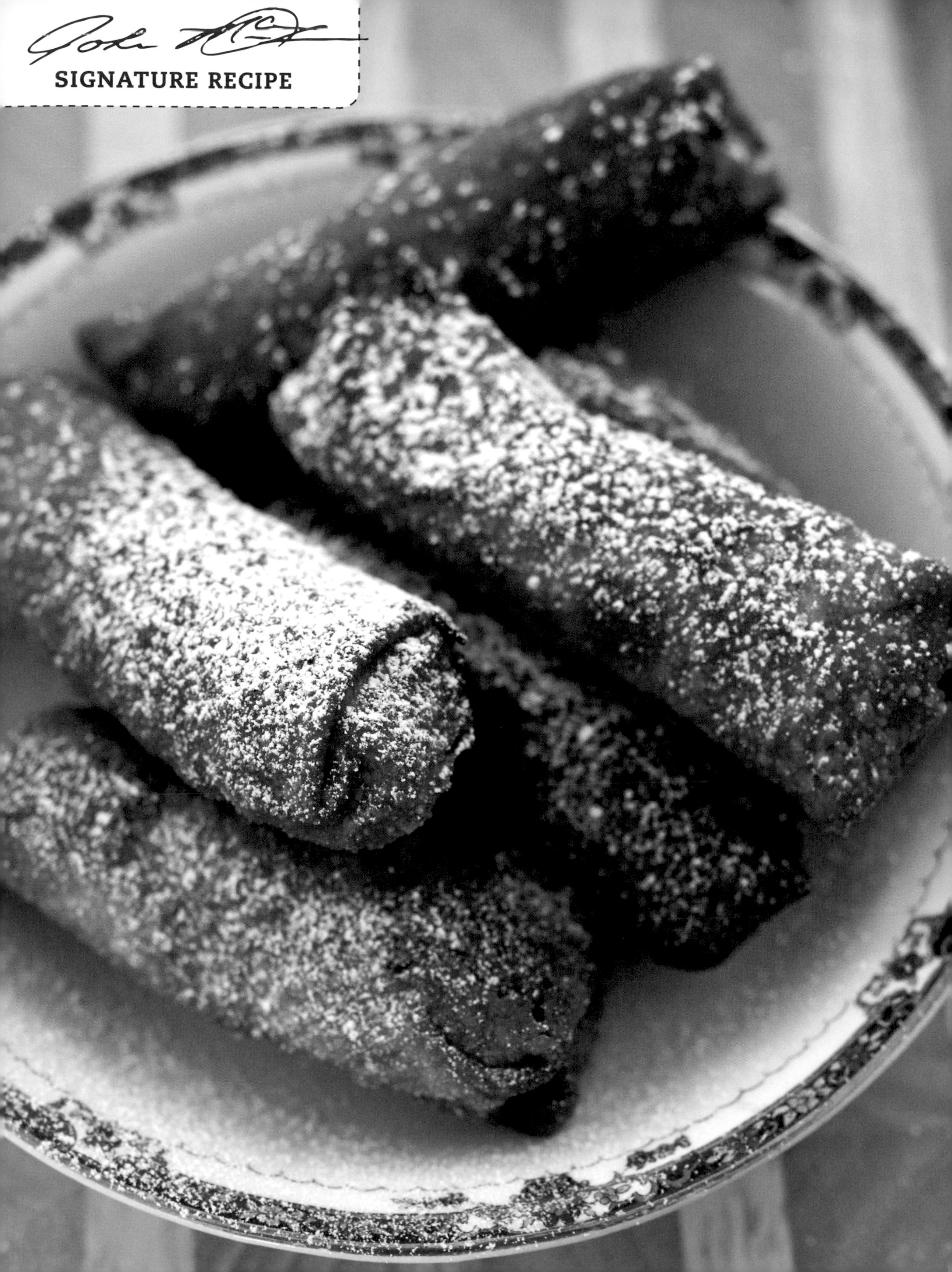

MASTERBUILT COURT PEAR PIES
Serves 4 to 6

In 2007, Masterbuilt purchased a new facility on Crown Circle in Columbus, GA. It was a proud moment in our history when the city of Columbus renamed the street Masterbuilt Court. In our parking lot, we have a pear tree that blooms and overflows with pears each year. We share these pears with our employees and the deer that walk up from the woods behind our office. These pear pies are good served alone with powdered sugar, but I highly recommend serving them on top of a scoop of vanilla ice cream.

You'll Need

- 3 tablespoons butter
- 3 pears, peeled and diced (about 2 cups)
- 2 tablespoons light brown sugar
- 1 teaspoon ground cinnamon
- 1/2 teaspoon ground nutmeg
- 1 gallon cooking oil
- 6 egg roll wrappers
- Cinnamon sugar or confectioners' sugar (optional)

Instructions

1. In a large skillet, heat butter over medium heat. Add pears and cook, stirring frequently, for 5 minutes. Add brown sugar, cinnamon and nutmeg. Reduce heat to medium-low and cook for 10 to 15 minutes or until softened. If liquid cooks down and additional liquid is needed, add 1 tablespoon water at a time. Set aside.

2. Fill deep fryer halfway with oil and heat to 350°F.

3. Divide pear mixture evenly among wrappers. Fold one corner of wrapper over filling, tucking tip of corner under filling. Pull side corners over the middle and roll entire pie toward the last remaining corner. Lightly brush remaining corner with water, press gently and seal.

4. Fry pies in batches, turning once, for 2 to 2 1/2 minutes or until golden brown. Use a metal slotted spoon to transfer to paper towels to drain. Serve immediately with cinnamon sugar or confectioners' sugar.

Our family with city officials on the day Masterbuilt Court was named.

LOADED BAKED POTATO BITES
Makes 12 to 16

Any recipe that you can prep in advance and freeze makes life a lot easier. You can freeze these baked potato balls before dipping them in the batter. Once you take them out of the freezer to batter and fry, let them stand at room temperature while you are heating your oil. Be sure to add about 2 more minutes to the frying time. These loaded baked potato balls are a little piece of heaven — cheesy, ooey, gooey and dadgum good!

Instructions

1.   Preheat oven to 400°F. Place potatoes directly on oven rack and bake for 1 hour or until tender. Let cool slightly and mash. You can leave the skin on or off — your preference. If you leave the skin on, make sure you mash into small pieces.

2.   Fill deep fryer halfway with oil and heat to 350°F.

3.   In a large bowl, combine potatoes, cheese, bacon, chives and salt, mixing well. Shape into 1 1/2-inch balls.

4.   In a large bowl, combine flour and baking powder. Stir in eggs and milk, mixing well. Dip potatoes in egg mixture and fry in batches for 5 to 6 minutes or until golden brown. Use a metal slotted spoon to transfer to paper towels to drain. Serve immediately with sour cream and chives, if using.

You'll Need

- 1 pound baking potatoes (about 2 large)

- 1 gallon cooking oil

- 1 1/4 cups shredded sharp Cheddar cheese

- 4 slices bacon, cooked and crumbled

- 1 tablespoon chopped fresh chives

- 1 teaspoon kosher salt

- 1 cup all-purpose flour

- 1 teaspoon baking powder

- 2 eggs, lightly beaten

- 1/2 cup milk

- Sour cream and chives (optional)

KIDS CORN DOGS
Serves 16

Who doesn't love corn dogs?! These corn dogs are a kid-pleasing dish, but don't let the name fool you. In our house, being a kid has nothing to do with your age. I've heard it said before, "growing old is not an option, growing up is!" I choose not to grow up, and my wife and kids would give an AMEN to that! If you have some little kids in your crowd, halve the skewers and hot dogs for mini versions of this recipe.

You'll Need

- 16 (10-inch) wooden skewers, soaked in water for 30 minutes
- 1 cup all-purpose flour
- 1 cup yellow cornmeal
- 2 tablespoons granulated sugar
- 1 tablespoon baking powder
- 1/8 teaspoon freshly ground black pepper
- 1 egg, lightly beaten
- 1 cup milk
- 1 gallon cooking oil
- 2 (each 11-ounce) packages hot dogs
- Ketchup
- Mustard

Instructions

1. In a large bowl, combine flour, cornmeal, sugar, baking powder and pepper. Stir in egg and milk.

2. Fill deep fryer halfway with oil and heat to 375°F.

3. Soak wooden skewers in water for 30 minutes. Insert wooden skewers into hot dogs. Roll hot dogs in batter until well coated. Fry 2 or 3 corn dogs at a time for 2 minutes or until golden brown. Use a metal slotted spoon to transfer to paper towels to drain. Serve with your favorite condiments.

*The kids and I are growing up.
Or maybe not!*

Top Left: *As kids we always had a boat and fished with my dad.*

Top Right: *I still love spending time with the Ole' Man out on the water even if we don't catch anything.*

Bottom: *Lisa and I have a friendly rivalry on team spirit day at Masterbuilt.*

CATFISH FINGERS

Serves 6

My dad, aka "PawPaw," is one dadgum fish-fryin' fool! When I was growing up, we would fish for brim, crappie and catfish. We would catch 'em, clean 'em and cook 'em. There's nothing better than spending time with the world's greatest dad, the King of the Fish Fry!

Instructions

1. Fill deep fryer halfway with oil and heat to 350°F.

2. In a large shallow dish, combine flour, 1 1/2 teaspoons of salt and pepper. In another large shallow dish, whisk together eggs and milk. In a third, combine cracker crumbs and cornmeal. Lightly salt fish fillets with remaining 1 1/2 teaspoons of salt. Dredge fish in flour, dip in egg mixture and coat well in cracker mixture.

3. Fry fish in batches, turning once, for 3 to 4 minutes or until golden. Use a metal slotted spoon to transfer to paper towels to drain. Drizzle with lemon juice and serve immediately with cocktail or tartar sauce, if using.

You'll Need

- 1 gallon cooking oil
- 1 cup all-purpose flour
- 3 teaspoons kosher salt, divided
- 3/4 teaspoon freshly ground black pepper
- 2 eggs, lightly beaten
- 1/2 cup milk
- 1 1/2 cups crushed crackers (about 40), such as saltines
- 1 cup yellow cornmeal
- 2 pounds catfish fillets, cut into 1-inch strips
- Lemon juice
- Cocktail or tartar sauce (optional)

LISA'S JALAPEÑO CHEESE GRITS

Serves 4

Hands-down, one of the best cooks at Masterbuilt is my assistant, Lisa. She does a fantastic job organizing our employee meals and events and everyone looks forward to her cooking. One of her most popular dishes is Jalapeño Cheese Grits. They disappear so fast, you won't get an opportunity for a second helping! You won't attend a fish fry in the South without seeing a big ol' pot of cheese grits beside the fish. We couldn't give you a fried fish recipe without sharing a cheese grits recipe, and there's no better grits recipe than Lisa's.

Instructions

1. Cook grits according to package directions. In a large bowl, combine grits, cheese, butter, if using, jalapeños, Worcestershire sauce to taste, garlic powder and salt and pepper to taste. Stir in eggs.

2. Meanwhile, preheat oven to 350°F.

3. Place grits mixture in a 12- by 9-inch baking dish sprayed with vegetable spray. Bake in preheated oven for 50 minutes to 1 hour until firm.

You'll Need

- 4 servings of grits
- 1 cup grated sharp Cheddar cheese (more if desired)
- 1/2 stick butter (1/4 cup) (optional)
- 2 tablespoons chopped jalapeños or more
- 1 to 2 teaspoons Worcestershire sauce
- 1 teaspoon garlic powder
- Salt and freshly ground black pepper
- 2 eggs, beaten

My wife's green bean casserole is to die for! I request it as a side dish as often as possible. Since I don't have oven-baked recipes in this book, Tonya decided to try a new way to serve up her green beans — deep-fried! Now that I've tried these green beans with the chipotle dipping sauce, I'm adding another side dish to my request list! (P.S. If you want a copy of her green bean casserole recipe, contact us at www.dadgumthatsgood.com.)

Top: *Tonya on camera trying her hand at an infomercial testimonial.*
Middle: *She loves helping me at all of my cooking events. She doesn't even mind scrubbing a pot (but I do).*
Bottom: *Tonya loves traveling with me and getting to help eat all of our dadgum good food.*

TONYA'S GREEN BEANS WITH CHIPOTLE DIPPING SAUCE

Serves 6 to 8

Instructions

1. In a large bowl, combine flour, salt to taste, baking powder and baking soda. Add club soda and olive oil, mixing well.

2. Fill deep fryer halfway with oil and heat to 350°F.

3. **Chipotle Dipping Sauce:** In a food processor, blend together sour cream, mayonnaise, lime juice, chipotle peppers, garlic and chili powder until smooth.

4. Dip green beans in batter mixture. Fry green beans for 2 minutes or until golden brown. Use a metal slotted spoon to transfer to paper towels to drain. Serve immediately with sauce.

You'll Need

- 1 cup all-purpose flour
- 1/2 to 1 teaspoon kosher salt
- 1/4 teaspoon baking powder
- 1/4 teaspoon baking soda
- 1 cup club soda
- 2 teaspoons olive oil
- 3 cups fresh green beans, ends trimmed
- 1 gallon cooking oil

Chipotle Dipping Sauce

- 2/3 cup sour cream
- 6 tablespoons mayonnaise
- 6 tablespoons fresh lime juice
- 2 tablespoons canned chipotle peppers
- 2 cloves garlic, minced
- 1/2 teaspoon chipotle chili powder

SIGNATURE RECIPE

TRIPLE-TAKE STEAK FINGERS
Serves 8

These steak fingers are so dadgum good, they deserved a triple-take! Make your own tray of steak fingers for your guests to snack on while tailgating at home. When we tested in our kitchen, I pulled out some white bread and mayonnaise and made a steak finger sandwich. For my wife, Tonya, we put them on a salad with blue cheese dressing. Any way you like it, these steak fingers are a sure crowd pleaser!

Instructions

1. Fill deep fryer halfway with oil and heat to 350°F.

2. In a small bowl, combine 1 teaspoon of garlic powder, 1/2 teaspoon of salt and 1/4 teaspoon of pepper. Season steak fingers with spice mixture.

3. In a shallow dish, combine eggs and milk. In another large shallow dish, combine bread crumbs and remaining 1 teaspoon of garlic powder, 1/2 teaspoon of salt and 1/4 teaspoon of pepper. Dip steak strips in egg mixture and then dredge in bread crumbs.

4. Fry steak slices in batches, turning once, for 2 minutes or until golden brown. Use a metal slotted spoon to transfer to paper towels to drain. Serve immediately with your favorite dipping sauce.

You'll Need

- 1 gallon cooking oil
- 2 teaspoons garlic powder, divided
- 1 teaspoon kosher salt, divided
- 1/2 teaspoon freshly ground black pepper, divided
- 1 pound flank or round steak, cut into 1 1/2-inch slices
- 2 eggs, lightly beaten
- 3 tablespoons milk
- 1 1/4 cups seasoned bread crumbs
- Dipping Sauces (optional) Ranch dressing Honey mustard Barbecue sauce Steak sauce

One of our local attractions is Callaway Gardens in Pine Mountain, Georgia. We participated in their Harvest Moon Festival — an event that was all about farm-to-table with live cooking demos and entertainment. On the opening night, we had the privilege of meeting and dining with Claire Robinson from the Food Network. She is known for her simple recipes with 5 ingredients and I loved her cooking philosophy. She encouraged everyone to kick off their shoes when they got home each day and get comfy in the kitchen. She also said to make each dish according to the recipe the first time, then mix it up and make it your own. As I've traveled and met some really cool people, I love taking these pieces of advice home to my own kitchen. Claire was gracious enough to share one of her recipes for my book. I hope you enjoy her Sweet Potato Fritters.

Top: Me and Claire Robinson at the Harvest Moon Festival.

Middle: Thumbs-up from me, Tonya, Claire and our friends Gary and Alicia.

CLAIRE'S SWEET POTATO FRITTERS
Makes 18 to 24

Instructions

1. Fill deep fryer halfway with oil and heat to 365°F.

2. In a large bowl, using a hand mixer, combine sweet potato, ricotta, sugar and salt and pepper to taste until smooth. Fold in flour, a little at a time, until just combined.

3. Drop heaping teaspoons of mixture into hot oil in batches and fry, turning as needed to brown evenly, for 1 to 2 minutes or until golden brown. Use a metal slotted spoon to transfer to paper towels to drain. Dust with confectioners' sugar and a pinch of salt.

You'll Need

- Corn oil for frying
- 1 cup mashed, roasted and peeled sweet potatoes
- 1 cup whole milk fresh ricotta
- 1/4 cup confectioners' sugar, plus more for dusting
- Kosher salt and freshly cracked peppercorns
- 1/2 cup self-rising flour

PORK EGG ROLLS
Makes 8 to 10

This recipe gives you another opportunity to get creative in the kitchen. Although it calls for pork, you can add shrimp or chicken — or even leave the meat out and make veggie egg rolls. Just make sure you fully cook the meat before placing in the egg roll wrappers. These make a tasty appetizer or serve them up with rice and stir-fried veggies for a complete meal.

Instructions

1. Fill deep fryer halfway with oil and heat to 350°F.

2. In a large nonstick skillet over medium heat, cook pork for 2 minutes or until meat crumbles. Drain. Add cabbage, mushrooms, bean sprouts, green onions, soy sauce, garlic powder and pepper and cook for 4 minutes or until vegetables are tender.

3. Spoon 1/3 cup meat mixture in center of each egg roll wrapper. Fold top corner of wrapper over filling, tucking tip of corner under filling. Fold left and right corners over filling. Lightly brush remaining corner with water and tightly roll filled end toward remaining corner and press gently to seal.

4. Fry egg rolls in batches, turning once, for 2 minutes or until golden. Use a metal slotted spoon to transfer to paper towels to drain. Serve immediately. Serve with sauces, if using.

You'll Need

- 1 gallon cooking oil
- 1 pound ground pork
- 4 cups finely shredded cabbage
- 1 (8-ounce) package mushrooms, chopped
- 1 cup fresh bean sprouts, chopped
- 1/4 cup chopped green onions, white and green parts
- 4 tablespoons low-sodium or regular soy sauce
- 1/2 teaspoon garlic powder
- 1/4 teaspoon freshly ground black pepper
- 1 (16-ounce) package egg roll wrappers
- Hot mustard or sweet and sour sauce (optional)

FRIED CAULIFLOWER WITH DIPPING SAUCE

Serves 8 to 10

As we tested our way through recipes for this book, a couple of them completely took me by surprise. This recipe for fried cauliflower far exceeded my expectations. The cayenne pepper in the batter gave it a kick and the cauliflower florets held up nicely while frying. You may want to consider trimming down the larger florets so your guests will have nice bite-size portions. The dipping sauce adds a cool complement to this recipe. When paired together, they make a dadgum good combo.

Instructions

1. Fill deep fryer halfway with oil and heat to 350°F.

2. In a medium shallow bowl, combine eggs and milk. In another shallow bowl, combine flour, oregano, paprika, salt, and cayenne to taste. Add egg mixture to flour mixture, mixing well.

3. **Dipping Sauce:** In a small bowl, combine yogurt, cucumber, garlic, mint, dill, lemon juice, olive oil and salt. Cover and refrigerate until ready to serve or for up to 1 day.

4. Dip cauliflower into batter and fry in batches, turning occasionally if needed, for 5 to 6 minutes or until golden. Use a metal slotted spoon to transfer to paper towels to drain. Serve immediately. Serve with dipping sauce.

You'll Need

- 1 gallon cooking oil
- 2 large eggs, lightly beaten
- 1 1/4 cups milk
- 1 1/4 cups all-purpose flour
- 2 teaspoons dried oregano
- 1 teaspoon paprika
- 1 teaspoon kosher salt
- 1/4 to 1/2 teaspoon cayenne pepper
- 2 (each 10-ounce) packages cauliflower florets (about 3 1/2 cups)

Dipping Sauce

- 1 (6-ounce) container plain yogurt
- 1/2 cup diced cucumber
- 1 clove garlic, finely minced
- 1 tablespoon chopped fresh mint
- 1 tablespoon chopped fresh dill
- 1 teaspoon fresh lemon juice
- 1 teaspoon olive oil
- 1/8 teaspoon kosher salt

Everyone in my family knows that I love corn. Boiled corn, steamed corn, fried corn, grilled corn, smoked corn — you name it! This recipe marries together two of my favorite things — corn and hush puppies. Much fancier people than me call them fritters. No matter what you call them, they are dadgum good!

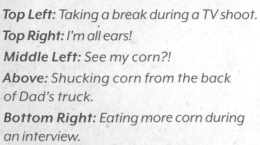

Top Left: *Taking a break during a TV shoot.*
Top Right: *I'm all ears!*
Middle Left: *See my corn?!*
Above: *Shucking corn from the back of Dad's truck.*
Bottom Right: *Eating more corn during an interview.*

JOHN'S CORN FRITTERS
Makes 15 to 20

Instructions

1. Fill deep fryer halfway with oil and heat to 350°F.

2. In a small bowl, combine corn, egg and milk. In a large bowl, combine flour, sugar, baking powder, salt and pepper. Add egg mixture to flour mixture, stirring to combine.

3. Drop batter by tablespoonfuls into hot oil and fry in batches for 6 to 8 minutes or until golden brown. You should see them turn on their own after about 2 to 3 minutes, but help them turn, if needed. Use a metal slotted spoon to transfer to paper towels to drain. Serve immediately.

You'll Need

- 1 gallon cooking oil
- 1 (12-ounce) can whole kernel corn
- 1 egg, lightly beaten
- 1/3 cup milk
- 1 1/4 cups all-purpose flour
- 1 tablespoon granulated sugar
- 1 teaspoon baking powder
- 1/2 teaspoon kosher salt
- 1/4 teaspoon freshly ground black pepper

My brother Don and I have been working together since 1973. We've worked hard, played hard and cooked a lot of dadgum good food all over the world. We were testing out some coconut shrimp recipes while writing this book and couldn't find one that met our standards. Remembering that Don makes the best shrimp tempura around, we decided to try his recipe with added coconut. It was a home run! After all these years, we still make a good team. Just don't tell him I stole his recipe!

Top: *Playing (I mean working) hard at QVC.*

Middle: *As boys, Don and I played hard on our motorcycles.*

Bottom: *Working (I mean playing) hard at "Fox and Friends."*

DON'S COCONUT SHRIMP
Serves 8

Instructions

1. Fill deep fryer halfway with oil and heat to 350°F.

2. In a large bowl, combine tempura mix and cold water using a wire whisk. Be sure to add the cold water slowly, a small amount at a time. The batter should be thin. In a separate shallow dish, combine panko and coconut. Place all-purpose flour in a sifter.

3. Dust shrimp lightly with all-purpose flour. Dredge in tempura batter, then roll in panko and coconut mixture.

4. Fry shrimp in batches, turning once, for 2 to 3 minutes or until golden. Use a metal slotted spoon to transfer to paper towels to drain. Serve immediately.

You'll Need

- 1 gallon cooking oil

- 1 cup tempura batter mix (no egg)

- 1 to 1 1/4 cups cold water

- 1 cup panko bread crumbs

- 1 cup sweetened flaked coconut

- 1/2 cup all-purpose flour

- 1 1/2 pounds large shrimp, peeled

We were testing jalapeño hush puppy recipes to complement the fish recipes in this cookbook. We tried many recipes and they all failed to meet the standard of PawPaw's hush puppies from our first cookbook. PawPaw is my dad, Dawson McLemore. He makes the best hush puppies ever and, truth be told, my momma said he stole that hush puppy recipe from her! Since there aren't any hush puppies like Dawson's hush puppies, we decided to add some "fire" to his recipe for this book. Enjoy this version of the Ole' Man's hush puppies. Since he stole the recipe from Momma, I'm sure he won't mind that we stole it again from him!

Top Left: *Sharing a hug with momma.*

Top Right: *Dawson frying up some hush puppies in the good ole days.*

Above: *He still fries up some dadgum good hush puppies.*

DAWSON'S FIRED-UP HUSH PUPPIES
Serves 6 to 8

Instructions

1. Fill deep fryer halfway with oil and heat to 350°F.

2. In a medium bowl, combine cornmeal, flour, baking soda, egg, onion and jalapeños. Stir in buttermilk until the consistency is thick enough to form golf ball-size hush puppies.

3. Drop the batter, 1 tablespoon at a time, into the hot oil. Dip the spoon into a glass of water to clean it after each hush puppy is dropped into the oil. Fry hush puppies, turning once, for 3 to 4 minutes or until golden brown. Once hush puppies are done, use a metal slotted spoon to transfer to paper towels to drain until ready to serve.

You'll Need

- 1 gallon cooking oil
- 2 cups yellow cornmeal
- 1/2 cup self-rising flour
- 1/16 teaspoon baking soda
- 1 large egg, lightly beaten
- 1/4 cup chopped yellow onion
- 1/4 cup chopped jalapeños
- 1 1/2 cups buttermilk

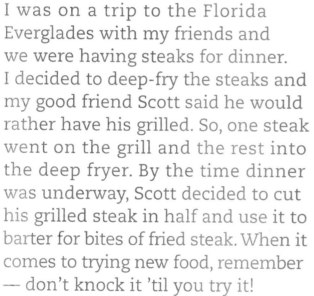

I was on a trip to the Florida Everglades with my friends and we were having steaks for dinner. I decided to deep-fry the steaks and my good friend Scott said he would rather have his grilled. So, one steak went on the grill and the rest into the deep fryer. By the time dinner was underway, Scott decided to cut his grilled steak in half and use it to barter for bites of fried steak. When it comes to trying new food, remember — don't knock it 'til you try it!

Top Left: *On an airboat in the Florida Everglades with J-Mac.*
Top Right: *J-Mac caught an alligator!*
Middle: *Dadgum good food with Scott.*
Bottom: *I decided to be a little more daring.*

DEEP-FRIED STEAK

Serves 2

Instructions

1. Fill deep fryer halfway with oil and heat to 350°F.

2. Generously season steaks on both sides.

3. Deep-fry the steaks for 3 minutes for rare, 4 minutes for medium results, 5 minutes for well-done. Using metal tongs remove steak carefully from hot oil and transfer to paper towels to drain. Please note: Per 1/4 of an inch thickness, add one minute to the recipe (example: 1 1/2 inch steaks will take 6 minutes for medium).

You'll Need

- 1 gallon cooking oil

- 2 rib-eye steaks (each 1-inch thick)

- 1 tablespoon steak seasoning or rub

SMOKIN' FRIED TURKEY

Serves 6 to 12

Our Masterbuilt fans are some of the most loyal and dedicated fans out there. They love to BBQ and love to show off their food. Bill is one of those fans and he shared his recipe for frying up a smoked turkey. That's one of the great things about our fans — they sometimes think to try recipes and techniques we haven't even tried yet! This 2-step process of smoking a turkey then deep-frying it may seem a bit off-the-wall, but I promise the results are dadgum good.

Instructions

1. Fill water tray 1/3 full with a 50/50 mixture of apple juice and water. Preheat smoker to 275°F.

2. Rinse and dry thawed turkey. Using a marinade injection syringe, inject turkey with one jar of Butterball Buttery Creole marinade. Season outside and inside of turkey with Butterball Cajun Seasoning, rubbing it into the skin.

3. Place turkey on middle rack in smoker and close the door. Smoke for 2 hours.

4. Remove turkey from smoker, and re-inject with 8 ounces of marinade. Place turkey, breast side up, in fryer basket. Slowly lower basket into hot oil, being careful not to splatter hot oil. Fry turkey for 2 minutes per pound. Lift basket from the hot oil slowly. Insert a meat thermometer in the meaty part of the breast; turkey is done when it reads 165°F. If the turkey is not done, lower it carefully back into the oil for an additional 5 minutes. Once the turkey reaches the desired temperature (minimum 165°F), remove from oil.

5. Let turkey rest and drain in fryer basket for 10 minutes before removing for carving. The turkey can remain in the basket to cool until ready to serve.

6. Based on the weight of your turkey, you will need to adjust the total cooking time, for deep-frying for 2 minutes per pound.

You'll Need

- 50/50 mixture apple juice and water

- 1 fresh or frozen whole turkey, thawed if frozen (10 to 12 pounds)

- 1 (16-ounce) jar + (8 ounces) Butterball Buttery Creole Injection Marinade or your favorite marinade

- 3.7-ounce Butterball Cajun Seasoning or your favorite Cajun seasoning

- Seasonings and marinades (optional) (see below)

- 2 gallons cooking oil, preferably peanut oil

Additional Seasoning/ Marinade Options:

We highly recommend the Butterball Seasoning Kit with the Buttery Creole Marinade and Cajun Seasoning, but there are other options if you prefer a milder flavor. You can inject the turkey with the marinade of your choice or chicken broth. Season the outside and inside of the turkey with salt and pepper, rubbing it into the skin. Place 8 to 10 pats of butter underneath the skin. You can also tuck several bay leaves underneath the skin.

▶ suggested wood

HICKORY, MESQUITE, APPLE OR PECAN

FRIED JAMBALAYA RICE CAKES
Serves 8 to 12

This recipe easily goes from side dish to main dish with the addition of sausage or shrimp. You can get the kids involved in making the rice cakes — they'll love getting their hands messy! Finish them off with the Rémoulade Sauce from page 58.

Instructions

1. Melt butter in a large saucepan over medium-high heat. Add onions, bell pepper and garlic and cook, stirring constantly, for 4 minutes. Stir in chicken broth and Cajun seasoning. Bring to a boil, then stir in rice. Return to a boil. Reduce heat and simmer, covered, for 20 minutes or until tender. Remove from heat (do not uncover) and let stand for 30 minutes. Pour rice onto baking sheets and let cool completely.

2. In a large bowl, combine rice mixture, eggs and flour, stirring well. (At this point, you could stir in the optional ingredients of chopped cooked shrimp and/or chopped precooked smoked sausage.) Using a 2 1/2-inch biscuit cutter or a 1/2 cup dry measuring cup as a mold, press to form small cakes. Dust with flour.

3. Place cakes on a baking sheet and cover with waxed paper. Refrigerate for 30 minutes or until chilled.

4. Meanwhile, fill deep fryer halfway with oil and heat to 350°F. Fry 4 or 5 cakes at a time, turning once, for 3 or 4 minutes or until golden. Use a metal slotted spoon to transfer to paper towels to drain.

You'll Need

- 1/4 cup butter

- 1 cup finely chopped yellow onions

- 1/2 cup finely chopped red bell pepper

- 1 tablespoon minced garlic

- 4 1/2 cups chicken broth or water

- 1 teaspoon Butterball Cajun Seasoning or Cajun seasoning of your choice

- 2 cups uncooked rice (your favorite type)

- 3 large eggs, lightly beaten

- 1 1/2 cups all-purpose flour

- Chopped shrimp and/or chopped precooked smoked sausage (optional)

- 1 gallon cooking oil, preferably peanut oil

Left: Serving up donuts at "The Daily Buzz."
Below: Donut eating contest.

When we traveled around the country on our book tour for *"DADGUM That's Good!"*™, we loved cooking at television/radio studios and feeding the crew. Anytime we made our fried donuts, they disappeared within minutes. We use canned biscuits to make our donuts and our original recipe called for drizzling them with sweetened condensed milk and dusting with powdered sugar. As dadgum good as those tasted, they were a mess to make. Our DTG Road Crew decided to come up with a less messy way to serve up these tasty treats. Placing the hot donuts in a container or paper bag with cinnamon-sugar and giving them a shake was a quick and easy way to contain the mess and serve up some goodness to the crews. These donuts made us quite popular and we're sure they will do the same for you!

Middle: Fun with Lamar from the "Bob and Sheri Show."
Above: Making donuts with Tonya.

DTG ROAD TOUR DONUTS

Makes 20 to 40

Instructions

1. Fill deep fryer halfway with oil and heat to 350°F.

2. In a bowl, combine cinnamon and sugar and spread onto a plate.

3. Cut each biscuit in half or 1/4 portions. Fry biscuit pieces, turning once, for 3 to 4 minutes or until golden brown. Use a metal slotted spoon to transfer to paper towels to drain. While still hot, roll the donuts in the cinnamon-sugar mixture.

You'll Need

- 1 gallon cooking oil

- 1 tablespoon ground cinnamon

- 1 cup granulated sugar

- 1 can refrigerated home-style biscuits (10 to a can)

- 1 gallon cooking oil
- 2 1/2 cups white cornmeal
- 1 teaspoon granulated sugar
- 3/4 to 1 teaspoon kosher salt
- 1/2 teaspoon baking powder
- 1/4 cup half-and-half cream
- 1 1/4 cups boiling water
- Butter (optional)

HOT WATER CORNBREAD
Serves 12 to 16

This hot water cornbread is good served with soup or chili, but one of the best ways to eat cornbread is with collard greens. While on our book tour we made a stop at a television station in Memphis, TN. One of the crew members bragged that she made the best collard greens in the South. I'll let you in on her secret, but let's keep it between us! In a large pot, fry bacon slices in olive oil. When the bacon is done, sprinkle in 2 tablespoons of baking soda (this will froth up). Add your collard greens and wilt down each batch. Sprinkle with season-all salt to taste. Cook for 30 minutes and serve up with the cornbread.

Instructions

1.   Fill deep fryer halfway with oil and heat to 350°F.

2.   In a medium bowl, combine cornmeal, sugar, salt to taste and baking powder. Add half-and-half cream. Gradually add boiling water, stirring until batter is combined.

3.   Using a long spoon, drop batter by tablespoonfuls into hot oil and fry in batches, turning once, for 2 to 3 minutes or until golden brown. Use a metal slotted spoon to transfer to paper towels to drain. Serve immediately with butter, if using.

SPICY FRIED CHICKEN

Serves 4

When my wife and I started dating she was attending Auburn University and lived in a small apartment. She wanted to make fried chicken for me, so her mother prepped and breaded some chicken pieces and sent them with her in a plastic baggie. She pulled them out of the fridge and fried them up for dinner. This first attempt seemed to be a success and she placed the golden fried chicken on our plates. When I cut into the chicken, blood spilled all over the plate! It was raw in the center and did not cook through. We ended up going to a local restaurant to eat fried chicken fingers for dinner. Tonya and I have come a long way since those days at Auburn and we love cooking together. In fact, now our kids love to join in on the process. Whether it's a home-cooked meal or chicken fingers at a restaurant, as long as I'm eating with my family I'm a happy guy.

You'll Need

- 2 1/2 to 3 pounds chicken, assorted pieces
- 3/4 teaspoon kosher salt
- 1 teaspoon freshly ground black pepper
- 2 eggs
- 2 cups buttermilk
- 3 tablespoons hot sauce
- 1 gallon cooking oil
- 1 1/2 cups all-purpose flour
- 1 tablespoon crushed red pepper flakes
- 1 teaspoon baking powder
- 1 teaspoon garlic powder
- 1 teaspoon paprika
- 1 teaspoon dried thyme

Instructions

1. Sprinkle chicken with salt and pepper. In a large bowl, whisk together eggs, buttermilk and hot sauce and pour over chicken, turning to coat. Place in refrigerator for 30 to 60 minutes. Remove from fridge and let stand at room temperature for 10 minutes before breading.

2. Fill deep fryer halfway with oil and heat to 350°F.

3. In a large shallow dish, combine flour, red pepper flakes, baking powder, garlic powder, paprika and thyme. Remove chicken from buttermilk mixture. Dredge in flour mixture.

4. Fry chicken, turning as needed, until golden brown. Wings and drumsticks fry for 12 to 14 minutes, thighs for 14 to 16 minutes, breasts for 16 to 20 minutes. Use a metal slotted spoon to transfer to paper towels to drain. If you would like to spice it up even more, double the hot sauce and red pepper.

As a manufacturer of fish cookers, it's only natural that I would fish with my family. Some of my fondest memories have been made on fishing trips with my dad, my brother Don or my kids. Any day where you get to spend time with family and friends, catch your dinner and fry it up together is a dadgum good day in my book!

Top Left: *Don and I fishing in Canada.*
Top Right: *Dawson with a nice catch.*
Middle: *Don and I sturgeon fishing.*
Bottom: *Life is good when you get to fish with your kids.*

GROUPER SANDWICHES

Serves 4

Instructions

1. **Mayonnaise-Lime Topping:** In a medium bowl, combine mayonnaise, lime juice, pickles, onion, parsley and jalapeño. Cover and refrigerate until serving for up to 2 days.

2. Fill deep fryer halfway with oil and heat to 350°F.

3. Place buttermilk in large shallow dish. Add grouper and let stand for at least 15 minutes.

4. In a medium shallow dish, combine flour, garlic powder, salt and pepper. Remove fish from buttermilk and dredge in flour mixture.

5. Fry fish in batches for 6 to 8 minutes or until golden and fish flakes easily when tested with a fork. Use a spatula to make sure fillets don't stick to the bottom of the fryer or pan and transfer to drain on paper towels. Serve on buns with mayonnaise mixture and desired toppings.

You'll Need

Mayonnaise-Lime Topping

- 1/3 cup reduced-fat or regular mayonnaise
- 2 tablespoons fresh lime juice
- 1 tablespoon chopped sweet pickles
- 1 tablespoon chopped red or yellow onion
- 1 tablespoon chopped fresh Italian parsley
- 1 teaspoon chopped jalapeño (about 1/2)

- 1 gallon cooking oil
- 3/4 cup buttermilk
- 2 pounds fresh grouper fillets, cut into 4 equal pieces
- 1 1/2 cups all-purpose flour
- 1 teaspoon garlic powder
- 1 teaspoon sea salt
- 1/2 teaspoon freshly ground black pepper
- 4 sandwich buns, toasted
- Lettuce (optional)
- Tomato (optional)

When my son, John, came to work for Masterbuilt, having two John McLemores became a communication challenge. John has gone by many nicknames through the years — John Boy, Little John and J-Mac. The nickname J-Mac started when he was pitching in Little League baseball. To help with the confusion at the office, we decided to go with J-Mac. It's been a fun experience to see him grow as a man and learn the ropes at Masterbuilt. One of J-Mac's favorite foods is canned ravioli. It's not gourmet, but he loves it! When we decided to put deep-fried ravioli in the cookbook, I instantly thought of him. These flavorful bites are best served with warm marinara sauce. Even J-Mac can agree, these put canned ravioli to shame!

Middle: *J-Mac the pitching machine.*
Left: *And now...welcome to the real world. The University of Masterbuilt.*

J-MAC'S FRIED RAVIOLI
Serves 8 to 10

You'll Need

- 2 eggs, lightly beaten
- 1/2 cup milk
- 1 cup Italian-style bread crumbs
- 1 (9-ounce) package fresh ravioli (meat or cheese)
- 1 gallon cooking oil
- 1/4 cup grated Parmesan cheese
- Marinara sauce, warmed
- Freshly grated Parmesan cheese
- Chopped fresh parsley (optional)

Instructions

1. In a large shallow dish, combine eggs and milk. Place bread crumbs in another shallow bowl. Dip ravioli in egg mixture and then dredge in bread crumbs. Place on a large baking sheet and freeze for at least 15 minutes or until hard.

2. Fill deep fryer halfway with oil and heat to 350°F. Remove ravioli from freezer and fry in batches for 2 to 2 1/2 minutes or until golden brown. Use a metal slotted spoon to transfer to paper towels to drain. Sprinkle with grated Parmesan cheese. Serve immediately with marinara sauce and garnish with fresh Parmesan and parsley, if using.

FRIED APPLE PIES
Makes 4

Since we developed the first indoor electric turkey fryer at Masterbuilt, we've tried frying just about everything. One sure-fire hit at Masterbuilt and in the McLemore family is anything fried with a canned biscuit. We have filled these with canned fruit pie filling or fried them solo and topped with powdered sugar, sweetened condensed milk, chocolate syrup and so on. With this recipe you can make your own homemade apple pie filling and create a fried apple pie that puts any drive-through pie to shame!

You'll Need

- 3 tablespoons butter
- 2 Gala apples, chopped (about 3 cups)
- 3 tablespoons light brown sugar
- 1 teaspoon ground cinnamon
- 1 teaspoon grated lemon zest
- 1/2 (16.3-ounce) can refrigerated biscuits
- 1 gallon cooking oil
- Confectioners' sugar (optional)

Instructions

1.   In a large skillet over medium heat, melt butter. Add apples and cook, stirring frequently, for 2 to 4 minutes or until they begin to soften. Add brown sugar, cinnamon and lemon zest and cook for 8 to 10 minutes more. Set aside and let cool completely.

2.   On a lightly floured surface, roll out biscuits to form a 6-inch circle. Place 1/3 cup filling on each circle. Brush the edges with water. Fold the circle over to make a semicircle shape. Press edges together.

3.   Fill deep fryer halfway with oil and heat to 350°F.

4.   Fry apple pies in batches, turning once at 90 seconds, for 3 to 4 minutes or until golden brown. Use a metal slotted spoon to transfer to paper towels to drain. Sprinkle with confectioners' sugar, if using.

Yum! Soon to be a fried apple pie.

BANANA WONTONS
Makes 24

This recipe calls for wrapping the wontons in an egg roll–type fashion. If you're brave enough, you can try making a wonton "purse." Place the filling in the center of the wonton wrapper. Wet all four edges of the wrapper. Lift the top and bottom edges of the wrapper and press together from the top to about halfway down to seal. Bring the right and left edges together and twist to seal. Deep fry them until golden brown.

Instructions

1. Fill deep fryer halfway with oil and heat to 350°F.

2. Place one banana slice over each wrapper. Sprinkle each with 1/8 teaspoon of cinnamon and 1/2 teaspoon of brown sugar. Top with nuts, if using. Fold top corner of wrapper over filling, tucking tip of corner under filling. Fold left and right corners over filling. Lightly brush remaining corner with water and tightly roll filled end toward remaining corner; press gently to seal.

3. Fry wontons in batches, turning once, for 2 to 3 minutes or until golden brown. Use a metal slotted spoon to transfer to paper towels to drain. Serve immediately. Sprinkle with confectioners' sugar and cinnamon, if using.

You'll Need

- 1 gallon cooking oil

- 2 large bananas, thinly sliced (about 1/4 inch thick)

- 24 wonton wrappers

- 2 tablespoons ground cinnamon, divided

- 1/2 cup packed light brown sugar, divided

- 1 cup pecans, chopped, toasted (optional)

- 1/4 cup confectioners' sugar

- 1/4 cup ground cinnamon (optional)

We were raised on wild game — anything my dad would bring home — boar, deer, turkey, you name it! My mom cooked up whatever Dad brought home and we had no problem cleaning our plates. One of the ways Mom would draw out the "wild" taste of the meat was to soak it in buttermilk. Although chicken and pork aren't wild game, she used buttermilk on those as well, with dadgum good results.

Top: The Ole' Man has still "got game" when it comes to hunting.
Middle: J-Mac is ready for the hunt.
Bottom: The Ole' Man tags two nice eight pointers.

FRIED PORK CHOPS

Serves 4

The lemon pepper and rosemary in this recipe give the pork chops great flavor. I definitely recommend thin pork chops, which fry in about 2 1/2 to 3 1/2 minutes.

Instructions

1. Fill deep fryer halfway with oil and heat to 350°F.

2. In a large bowl, combine flour, rosemary, garlic powder, lemon pepper and 1 teaspoon of salt.

3. Lightly salt pork chops with remaining 1/2 teaspoon of salt. Place buttermilk in a large shallow dish. Dip pork chops in buttermilk and then dredge in flour mixture. Fry pork in batches, turning once, for 2 1/2 to 3 1/2 minutes or until golden brown. Use metal tongs to transfer to paper towels to drain. Serve immediately. Garnish with fresh rosemary, if using.

You'll Need

- 1 gallon cooking oil

- 1 cup all-purpose flour

- 2 tablespoons chopped fresh rosemary

- 1 teaspoon garlic powder

- 1 teaspoon lemon pepper

- 1 1/2 teaspoons kosher salt, divided

- 4 boneless skinless thin pork loin chops (about 1 1/2 pounds total)

- 1/2 cup buttermilk

- Fresh rosemary sprigs (optional)

SWEET POTATO FRIES WITH MAPLE PECAN BUTTER

Serves 4 to 6

You'll Need

- 1 gallon cooking oil
- 1 1/2 pounds sweet potatoes, cut into thin fries

Maple Pecan Butter

- 1/4 cup butter
- 3 tablespoons maple syrup
- 1/8 teaspoon ground cinnamon
- 1/8 teaspoon salt
- 1 tablespoon chopped pecans

While cooking our way through all of these recipes, we tried our hardest to go easy on the amount of food we ate. As you can imagine, over 130 recipes in a short period of time could really add to the waistline! Occasionally, we would have a hard time walking away from a particular recipe. The maple pecan butter was so dadgum good, we ate it straight out of the saucepan! We would highly recommend drizzling this over a big ol' scoop of vanilla ice cream.

Instructions

1. Fill deep fryer halfway with oil and heat to 350°F.

2. **Maple Pecan Butter:** In a small saucepan over low heat, combine butter, maple syrup, cinnamon and salt for 2 minutes or until butter is melted. Stir in pecans and cook 2 minutes more.

3. Fry sweet potatoes in batches for 4 to 6 minutes or until browned. Use a metal slotted spoon to transfer to paper towels to drain. Serve immediately with Maple Pecan Butter.

You'll Need

- 1 gallon cooking oil
- 1 1/2 cups all-purpose flour
- 1/2 cup yellow cornmeal
- 1 teaspoon baking powder
- 3/4 teaspoon kosher salt
- 2 cups ginger ale
- 12 whole mushrooms
- 1 cup baby carrots
- 2 yellow squash, thinly sliced
- Ranch salad dressing (optional)

FRIED VEGGIES

Serves 8

Although I will admit this is in no way a healthy dish, it is a creative way to get your guests to eat their veggies! A tray of these fried veggies make a crowd-pleasing appetizer. This recipe calls for using mushrooms, carrots and squash, but you can get creative and try other veggies in the mix. They are good when served with traditional Ranch salad dressing or one of the many other Ranch flavor variations on the salad dressing aisle at your local grocery store.

Instructions

1.   Fill deep fryer halfway with oil and heat to 350°F.

2.   In a large bowl, combine flour, cornmeal, baking powder and salt. Add ginger ale, mixing well. Set aside.

3.   Dip mushrooms, carrots and squash in batter and fry in batches, turning once if needed, for 3 to 4 minutes or until golden. Use a metal slotted spoon to transfer to paper towels to drain. Serve immediately. Serve with Ranch dressing, if using.

My wife, Tonya, and I were at a restaurant in Pine Mountain, Georgia, one day for lunch. She ordered a fried green tomato sandwich and went on and on about how good it tasted. My goal was to make a sandwich better than the restaurant. When testing this recipe, we made sure Tonya was the Chief Taste-Tester for the day. She gave the sandwich a thumbs-up and her seal of approval. Mission accomplished!

Top Left: *Tonya found the perfect gift for me! Thumbs-up is a signature move in our family.*

Top Right: *Bailey gives a "sassy" thumbs-up!*

Middle: *Brooke gives a hungry thumbs-up.*

Right: *J-Mac gives a shy little thumbs-up.*

THUMBS-UP FRIED GREEN TOMATO SANDWICHES WITH SPICY MAYONNAISE SPREAD

Serves 4

Instructions

1. **Spicy Mayonnaise Spread:** In a small bowl, combine mayonnaise, lemon juice, Dijon, bell pepper, pickle relish, green onions and hot sauce. Use immediately as a sandwich spread or cover and refrigerate for up to 2 days.

2. Fill deep fryer halfway with oil and heat to 350°F.

3. In a medium bowl, combine cornmeal, flour, panko, salt and pepper. Place eggs in a shallow dish. Dip tomatoes in egg and then in cornmeal mixture.

4. Fry tomatoes in batches, turning once, for 2 minutes or until lightly browned. Use a metal slotted spoon to transfer to paper towels to drain.

5. Place bread slices on a work surface. Spread 4 slices equally with mayonnaise mixture. Top equally with bacon, lettuce and green tomatoes. Top with remaining bread slices.

You'll Need

Spicy Mayonnaise Spread

- 1/2 cup sandwich spread mayonnaise mixture
- 1 tablespoon fresh lemon juice
- 1 tablespoon Dijon mustard
- 1 tablespoon chopped red bell pepper
- 2 teaspoons pickle relish
- 2 teaspoons chopped green onions, white and green parts
- 1/2 teaspoon hot sauce

- 1 gallon cooking oil
- 1/2 cup self-rising cornmeal
- 1/4 cup all-purpose flour
- 1/4 cup panko bread crumbs
- 1/4 teaspoon salt
- 1/4 teaspoon freshly ground black pepper
- 2 eggs, lightly beaten
- 2 green tomatoes, thinly sliced
- 8 slices sourdough bread (1/2-inch thick)
- 1/4 cup mayonnaise
- 4 slices bacon
- 1/2 cup arugula or mixed greens

SIGNATURE RECIPE

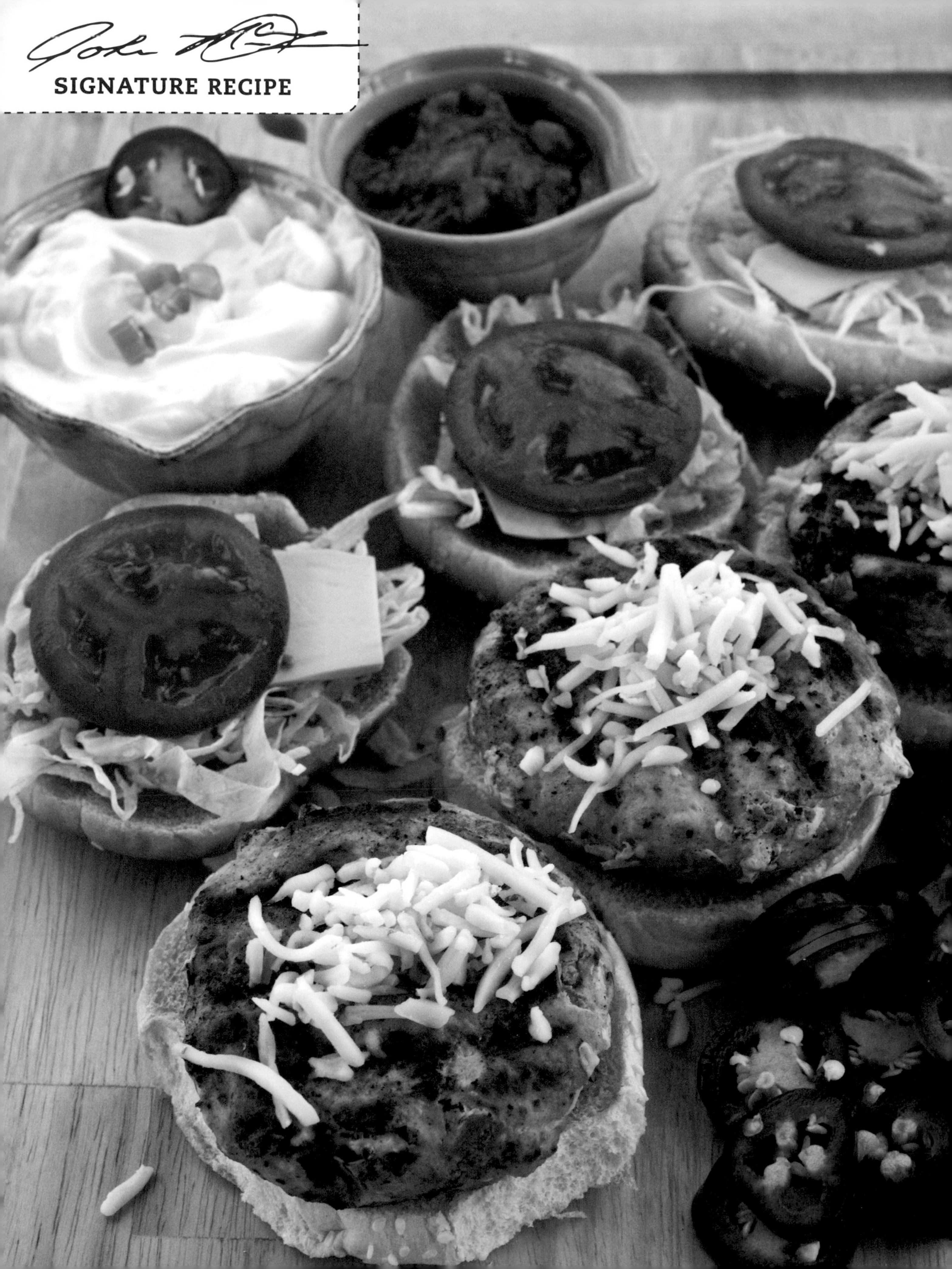

SOUTHWESTERN TURKEY BURGERS

Serves 4

Jeff is my General Manager at Masterbuilt. He makes a mean turkey burger that everyone raves about. When we tested this recipe, I knew I wanted Jeff to be the chief taste tester. I'm proud to say, he liked this recipe better than his! Chilling these burgers in the freezer is a key step in the process — it helps them keep their shape on the grill. The green chiles give these burgers flavor and a kick in the pants.

Instructions

1. Preheat lightly greased grill to 400°F (medium-high setting).

2. In a large bowl, combine turkey, lime juice, chili powder, oregano, cumin, salt, black pepper and green chiles, mixing well. Shape into 4 patties, each 3/4 inch thick, and spray both sides lightly with cooking spray. Place patties on a plate with a sheet of heavy-duty foil and chill, covered, in freezer for 1 hour.

3. Remove patties from freezer and grill, with grill lid closed, for 4 minutes on each side or until desired degree of doneness. Top with cheese during last minute of grilling. Serve burgers on buns with tomato and desired toppings.

You'll Need

- 1 1/4 pounds ground turkey
- 1 tablespoon fresh lime juice
- 1 1/2 teaspoons chili powder
- 1 1/2 teaspoons dried oregano
- 1 1/4 teaspoons ground cumin
- 3/4 to 1 teaspoon kosher salt
- 1/2 teaspoon freshly ground black pepper
- 1 (4 1/2-ounce) can chopped green chiles
- Vegetable cooking spray
- 4 slices or 1/2 cup shredded Monterey Jack cheese
- 4 hamburger buns, split and toasted
- 1 large tomato, thinly sliced
- Toppings (optional)
  Shredded lettuce
  Salsa
  Sour cream
  Avocado
  Chopped jalapeños

*Good times with my General Manager, Jeff.
He's the turkey burger king!*

You'll Need

- 1/2 cup melted butter
- 1/4 cup fresh lemon juice
- 1/4 cup Worcestershire sauce
- 2 cloves garlic, minced
- 2 tablespoons Old Bay seasoning
- 1 tablespoon lemon pepper
- 2 pounds large fresh shrimp, unpeeled
- Freshly chopped parsley (optional)
- French bread (optional)

SOUTHERN BARBECUED SHRIMP
Serves 4 to 6

In the South, we love to "sop" with biscuits or bread. What's sopping? Well, I'm sure it's not listed in a fancy manners book, but you simply take your bread and drag it across the juices/gravy on your plate and "sop" it up. These Southern Barbecued Shrimp create a sauce that is the ultimate sopping sauce. Our family got into an all-out sopping war over this one!

Instructions

1. In a large bowl, combine butter, lemon juice, Worcestershire sauce, garlic, Old Bay seasoning and lemon pepper. Add shrimp, tossing well. Let stand for at least 30 minutes or cover and refrigerate for up to 8 hours.

2. Preheat lightly greased grill to 400°F (medium-high setting).

3. Arrange 4 (12-inch long) sheets heavy-duty aluminum foil on a work surface. Divide shrimp evenly among sheets of foil. Gather sides of foil over shrimp to cover completely and crimp edges to seal packets. Place packets on preheated grill. Grill packets, with grill lid closed, for 4 to 5 minutes on each side or until shrimp turns pink. Top with parsley before serving and serve with French bread, if using. Serve immediately.

GRILLED STEAKS WITH SMOKED PAPRIKA

Serves 4

The smoked paprika in this recipe is a quick way to give smokey flavor to a grilled steak. If you've got some extra time to smoke some steaks, be sure to check out my recipe for Smoked Beef Filet Steaks on page 88.

Instructions

1. Preheat lightly greased grill to 400°F (medium-high setting).

2. In a small bowl, combine paprika, brown sugar, sea salt and pepper. Add olive oil, mixing well. Rub paprika mixture over steaks.

3. Grill steaks, with grill lid closed, for 3 to 4 minutes per side or until desired degree of doneness. See Doneness Chart to the right for temperatures. Serve with honey barbecue sauce, if using.

You'll Need

- 1 tablespoon smoked paprika
- 1 tablespoon dark brown sugar
- 1 teaspoon sea salt
- 1/2 teaspoon freshly ground black pepper
- 2 tablespoons olive oil
- 4 (1/2-inch thick) rib-eye steaks (about 2 pounds)
- Honey barbecue sauce (optional)

Doneness Chart

125°F Rare

135°F Medium-Rare

145°F Medium

155°F Medium-Well

165°F Well Done

I've had the privilege of appearing on "Fox and Friends" many times and love the folks on that team. One of the most fun people I've met is Judge Jeanine Pirro. She loved our food and graciously shared her family recipe for hummus. When I asked about being on her show she said, "You don't want to be on my show; It's about murder, mayhem and corruption! And unless there's a recipe worth killing over....." Gotta love her sense of humor! And, for the record, I really don't want to be on her show — I'll stick with cooking segments.

Top: *With Judge Jeanine at Fox News.*

Bottom: *Another great visit with Judge Jeanine at "Fox and Friends."*

GRILLED PITA WITH JUDGE JEANINE'S HUMMUS

Serves 8

Instructions

1. Preheat lightly greased grill to 350°F (medium setting).

2. Put garlic through a press and add 1/4 teaspoon of salt to it. Add tahini and lemon juice and mix together. In a food processor, blend chickpeas and garlic mixture for about 2 minutes, until a creamy texture. If consistency is too thick, add some of the reserved liquid from chickpeas. Transfer to a bowl. Cover and refrigerate for 2 hours or for up to 3 days. Serve hummus with grilled pita bread.

3. To grill pita, brush evenly with olive oil and sprinkle with remaining salt and paprika. Grill, with grill lid closed, over medium heat for 1 to 2 minutes on each side or until grill marks appear. Immediately transfer grilled pitas to a cutting board and slice each into six wedges or break into large pieces. Serve with hummus.

You'll Need

- 2 cloves garlic, peeled
- 1/2 teaspoon salt, divided
- 2 tablespoons tahini
- Juice of 1/2 lemon
- 1 (15-ounce) can chickpeas, rinsed and drained, 1/4 cup liquid reserved
- 1 bag pita bread, about 4 slices (5 1/2 to 6 inches in diameter)
- 2 tablespoons olive oil
- 1/4 teaspoon paprika

I started working with my dad at the ripe old age of 8. By the time I was 14, we had grown our family business and had many more employees. It became a little awkward at the office to refer to Dawson as "daddy," so I started calling him Old Man. He quickly let me know that he was "not old," so I changed it to Ole'. The name stuck, and he's been my Ole' Man ever since. When it comes to grilling steaks, no one does it like the Ole' Man. When I served him this steak recipe, he responded with "Son, that's a dadgum good steak!" I guess that means this one gets the Ole' Man's seal of approval!

Top Left: *The start of our grill business.*
Top Right: *My dad's a handsome fella!*
Middle: *Kiddin' around with the Ole' Man.*
Bottom: *Don, Dad, me and Momma.*

OLE' MAN'S STEAK
Serves 4

Instructions

1. Preheat lightly greased grill to 400°F (medium-high setting).

2. In a medium bowl, combine garlic, Heinz 57 Sauce, Worcestershire sauce and onion powder. Baste each steak with mixture. Place steaks in a large resealable plastic bag and marinate in the refrigerator for 2 to 3 hours.

3. Remove from marinade, discarding marinade. Place steaks on medium-high heat and grill, with grill lid closed, for 12 minutes (for medium), turning every 3 minutes. Cook to desired degree of doneness (see Doneness Chart to the right for temperatures). Sprinkle with garlic salt and pepper (don't miss this step) and remove from grill.

You'll Need

- 4 cloves garlic, minced
- 1/2 cup Heinz 57 Sauce
- 1/4 cup Worcestershire sauce
- 1 teaspoon onion powder
- 4 T-bone or Porterhouse steaks, cut 1 to 1 1/4 inches thick
- 2 teaspoons garlic salt
- 2 teaspoons black pepper

Doneness Chart

125°F Rare

135°F Medium-Rare

145°F Medium

155°F Medium-Well

165°F Well Done

You'll Need

- 1 1/2 pounds ground beef
- 8 hot dogs
- 16 slices bacon

BACON BURGER DOGS
Serves 8

The kids love hot dogs, the adults love burgers and everyone loves bacon, so these Bacon Burger Dogs are the perfect party food. Our kids play in the praise band at our church and work up a good appetite on rehearsal nights. We grilled up some Bacon Burger Dogs for the band one night and they were a huge hit! You can slice them in smaller portions and serve on slider buns with your favorite condiments. You can also deep-fry these for 5 minutes (with oil temp set to 325°F). Whether you grill them, fry them or serve them up on slider rolls, your guests will keep coming back for more!

Instructions

1. Preheat lightly greased grill to 350°F (medium setting).

2. Shape ground beef into 8 thin patties. Form patties around each hot dog and seal edges. Wrap 2 slices bacon around each hot dog. Secure with toothpicks. Place on top rack of grill/warming rack and grill, with grill lid closed, turning frequently, for 20 to 25 minutes or until internal temperature reaches 145°F. The bacon will create flare-ups, so don't leave unattended.

You'll Need

- 8 (6-inch) wooden skewers, soaked in water for 30 minutes

- 3 tablespoons fresh lime juice

- 1 teaspoon honey

- 1/4 teaspoon ground cinnamon

- 2 large ripe nectarines, pitted and cut into 1 1/2-inch pieces

- 1 cup (1 1/2-inch cubes) fresh pineapple

- 1 cup (1 1/2-inch cubes) honeydew melon

- 1 cup (1 1/2-inch cubes) cantaloupe

GRILLED FRUIT KABOBS

Serves 8

Grilled fruit is a quick, easy and unique treat. Use a high setting on your grill to caramelize the honey and cinnamon. You can also use peaches, plums or watermelon on these kabobs.

Instructions

1. Preheat lightly greased grill to 350°F (medium setting).

2. In a small bowl, combine lime juice, honey and cinnamon. Set aside.

3. Soak wooden skewers in water for 30 minutes. Thread nectarines, pineapple, honeydew and cantaloupe evenly on skewers. Drizzle lime mixture over fruit. Place kabobs on a grill rack and grill, with grill lid closed, for 3 to 4 minutes or until grill marks appear. Serve immediately.

BALSAMIC RIB-EYE STEAK SANDWICHES

Serves 4

As much as I love a good ol' grilled steak by itself, I'm always open for a creative way to serve it up to my guests. These steak sandwiches were a huge hit with our kids and their friends. The salty flavor of the sun-dried tomatoes in the mayonnaise, paired with the steak and blue cheese, made a dadgum good combination. You can cut these sandwiches into small portions and make your own sandwich tray, but be prepared for your guests to gobble them up quickly!

Instructions

1. In a resealable plastic bag, combine Worcestershire sauce and balsamic vinegar. Add steaks. Seal and refrigerate, turning occasionally, for at least 30 minutes or for up to 8 hours.

2. Preheat lightly greased grill to 400°F (medium-high setting).

3. Grill steaks, with grill lid closed, over medium-high heat for 5 minutes on each side or to desired degree of doneness (see Doneness Chart to the right). Slice across the grain into thin slices.

4. In a small bowl, combine mayonnaise and sun-dried tomatoes. Spread mayonnaise mixture on bread slices. Layer 4 bread slices with steak, lettuce, tomatoes and blue cheese and top with remaining bread slices.

You'll Need

- 1/4 cup Worcestershire sauce
- 1/4 cup balsamic vinegar
- 4 rib-eye steaks (each about 1 1/2 pounds)
- 1/3 cup low-fat or regular mayonnaise
- 1/4 cup chopped sun-dried tomatoes
- 8 Italian bread slices or large rolls, toasted
- 1 cup shredded lettuce or mixed salad greens
- 2 tomatoes, thinly sliced
- 4 tablespoons crumbled blue cheese or feta cheese

Doneness Chart
125°F Rare
135°F Medium-Rare
145°F Medium
155°F Medium-Well
165°F Well Done

CLASSIC BARBECUE CHICKEN
Serves 4

This classic BBQ sauce works well for marinating, basting and serving on the finished recipe. If you love pulled pork BBQ sandwiches, why not try a pulled chicken BBQ sandwich?! Use two forks to shred the chicken and serve on a bun with sauce, coleslaw and pickles.

Instructions

1. **Barbecue Sauce:** In a medium saucepan over medium heat, combine vinegar, ketchup, chili sauce, Worcestershire sauce, garlic and cayenne. Bring to a boil. Reduce heat and simmer, stirring occasionally, for 30 minutes. Let cool.

2. Place chicken in a large resealable plastic bag or shallow dish. Pour 1 cup of barbecue sauce over chicken and coat both sides. Cover and refrigerate for at least 30 minutes or for up to 2 hours. Reserve remaining sauce for later use.

3. Preheat lightly greased grill to 400°F (medium-high setting).

4. Remove chicken from barbecue sauce, discarding sauce. Grill chicken, with grill lid closed, for 20 to 35 minutes, turning every 4 minutes, until chicken is no longer pink inside and internal temperature reaches 165°F (cooking time will vary depending on size of chicken and whether bone-in or out). Brush chicken with 1 cup of reserved sauce during last 1 to 2 minutes of cooking. Let stand for 5 minutes. Serve with remaining 1 1/2 cups of reserved barbecue sauce.

You'll Need

Barbecue Sauce

- 1 1/2 cups apple cider vinegar
- 1 cup ketchup
- 1 cup chili sauce
- 2 tablespoons Worcestershire sauce
- 2 cloves garlic, minced
- 1/4 teaspoon cayenne pepper

- 4 boneless skinless chicken breasts (about 1 1/4 pounds) (see Bone-In Option below for using bone-in chicken instead)

Bone-In Option
You can also use bone-in chicken, which gets more tender results, but grill for 15 to 20 minutes longer or until internal temperature reaches 165°F.

CHICKEN AND VEGGIE KABOBS
Serves 6

Be sure to soak the skewers in water for at least 30 minutes to keep them from burning up as they grill. You may want to double-skewer the chicken and veggies. Using two wooden skewers will keep the ingredients from turning on a single skewer while you flip them for even grilling.

Instructions

1. Cut chicken into 1-inch chunks and place in a 1-gallon resealable plastic bag. In a medium bowl, combine salad dressing, Heinz 57 Sauce, A1 Steak Sauce, Worcestershire sauce, red wine vinegar, minced garlic, black peppercorns and garlic salt. Pour 1/2 of this mixture over the chicken in the bag, reserving 1/2 for veggies.

2. Place green and red bell peppers, onion, mushrooms and zucchini in another resealable bag and cover with remaining marinade. Seal bag and turn to coat veggies. Place chicken and veggies in refrigerator, turning occasionally, for several hours or make the day ahead and leave overnight in refrigerator, turning several times before cooking.

3. Preheat lightly greased grill to 400°F (medium-high setting). Soak wooden skewers in water for 30 minutes. Remove chicken and vegetables from marinade, discarding marinade, and thread onto skewers. Grill, with grill lid closed, for 6 minutes, then turn and grill for an additional 6 minutes or until internal temperature reaches 165°F and chicken is no longer pink inside.

You'll Need

- 6 (8-inch) wooden skewers, soaked in water for 30 minutes
- 6 large boneless skinless chicken breasts
- 1 (16-ounce) bottle Italian salad dressing
- 1 1/2 cups Heinz 57 Sauce
- 1 1/2 cups A1 Steak Sauce
- 1 cup Worcestershire sauce
- 1/4 cup red wine vinegar
- 4 teaspoons minced garlic
- 2 teaspoons cracked black peppercorns
- 1/2 teaspoon garlic salt
- 2 large green bell peppers, sliced into 1-inch pieces
- 1 large red bell pepper, sliced into 1-inch pieces
- 1 large Vidalia or sweet onion, sliced into 1-inch pieces
- 1 pound mushrooms, stemmed and halved
- 1 large zucchini, sliced into 1/4-inch slices

GRILLED CHICKEN FINGERS WITH PASTA

Serves 4

At the McLemore house, we love leftovers, which means we love any recipe that allows you to make extra portions and turn it into several different recipes. These juicy and flavorful chicken fingers are good when served as the main dish, but they also make a great addition to a salad or pasta dish. Add some shaved Parmesan, olive oil and fresh pepper to angel hair pasta and top with the chicken fingers or serve them over a salad with the Lemon Vinaigrette from page 181.

You'll Need

- 1/3 cup fresh lemon juice
- 1/4 cup olive oil
- 2 cloves garlic, minced
- 1 tablespoon chopped fresh basil
- 1 tablespoon chopped fresh rosemary
- 1/2 teaspoon kosher salt
- 1/4 teaspoon freshly ground pepper
- 4 boneless skinless chicken breasts, cut into thin strips
- 1 (1-pound) package angel hair pasta, cooked
- Lemon slices (optional)
- Fresh basil (optional)

Instructions

1. In a medium bowl, combine lemon juice, olive oil, garlic, basil, rosemary, salt and pepper. Place chicken in a resealable plastic bag. Pour lemon mixture over chicken. Seal and refrigerate, turning occasionally, for 1 to 4 hours.

2. Preheat lightly greased grill to 350°F (medium setting).

3. Grill chicken, with grill lid closed, for 4 minutes on each side or until internal temperature reaches 165°F or until no longer pink inside. Serve with lemon slices and fresh basil, if using, and pasta.

Honey-Citrus Sauce

- 1/3 cup honey

- 2 tablespoons fresh lemon juice

- 2 teaspoons chopped fresh mint (optional)

- 1/4 teaspoon vanilla extract

- 4 ripe firm peaches, cut in half and pits removed

- 3 ripe plums, cut in half and pits removed

- 2 tablespoons butter, melted

- Vanilla ice cream

GRILLED PEACHES AND PLUMS WITH HONEY-CITRUS SAUCE

Serves 4

When grilling fruit, especially a softer fruit like peaches and plums, you don't need to walk away from your grill. They cook quickly and need to be turned frequently. Watch them carefully and use caution with the butter because it will flare up. As an option, you can leave the mint out of the sauce.

Instructions

1. Preheat lightly greased grill to 350°F (medium setting).

2. **Honey-Citrus Sauce:** In a saucepan over medium-high heat, combine honey and lemon juice. Bring to a boil. Reduce heat to low and simmer for 5 minutes. Add chopped fresh mint, if using. Remove from heat and stir in vanilla.

3. Brush cut sides of peaches and plums with melted butter. Grill fruit, with grill lid closed, for 2 to 3 minutes on each side or until grill marks appear. Remove from grill and slice.

4. To serve, divide ice cream among 4 servings bowls. Top evenly with fruit and drizzle with sauce. Serve immediately.

I was a guest judge at the Battle of the Burgers in Atlanta, GA. This charity event benefited EMBRACED, an organization that provides orthopedic devices to those in need. It was a fun event and a bit of a challenge, as I had to sample 25 burgers! They served us every type of burger you could imagine — from waffle burgers with ice cream to mac 'n' cheese–stuffed burgers. One of the judges was Chef Rusty Hamlin from the Zac Brown Band crew. We ate ourselves miserable and had a blast! There's no need for you to eat through 25 burgers to find a winner; this recipe gets a blue ribbon from my crew.

Top: *The DTG team at Battle of the Burgers.*
Middle: *Full of burgers!*
Bottom: *Eating my way through over 20 burgers with Chef Rusty!*

GRILLED

You'll Need

- 1 1/2 pounds ground beef
- 1/4 cup finely chopped yellow onion (optional)
- 2 tablespoons Worcestershire sauce
- Salt and freshly ground black pepper
- 4 slices Swiss cheese
- 2 teaspoons olive oil
- 3 cups sliced fresh mushrooms
- 4 hamburger buns, split and toasted
- Toppings (optional)
  Avocado
  Lettuce
  Tomato
  Other toppings

SWISS MUSHROOM BURGERS
Serves 4

Instructions

1. Preheat lightly greased grill to 400°F (medium-high setting).

2. In a large bowl, combine beef, onion, if using, Worcestershire and 1/2 teaspoon pepper. Shape into 4 patties, each about 3/4 inch thick.

3. Grill burgers, with grill lid closed, for 4 minutes per side, then 2 minutes per side, for a total cooking time of 6 minutes per side. NOTE: Do not leave burgers on grill for a continuous 6 minutes per side or they will burn; you must turn after 4 minutes. Place Swiss on patties during the last 1 minute of grilling.

4. Meanwhile, place a skillet or large sheet of heavy-duty foil directly on grill. Add oil and mushrooms and sauté on medium-high heat until mushrooms are tender, 20 to 25 minutes. Season with salt and pepper to taste. Remove mushrooms from grill. Set aside.

5. Place burgers on buns, top with mushrooms and desired toppings and serve.

"DADGUM That's Good, Too!"™ | 171

GRILLED TUNA STEAKS
Serves 6

When you cook the marinade for these grilled tuna steaks, be sure to let it cool completely before pouring over the steaks. Otherwise, the hot marinade could cook the steaks in the fridge. The thickness of the steaks will determine the grilling time. Be sure to watch them carefully because tuna cooks quickly on the grill. You don't want to dry them out. I prefer my tuna steaks cooked to medium, but you can leave them rare and just sear on the outside if you like them that way.

Instructions

1. Place steaks in a disposable aluminum foil pan. In a medium saucepan, combine water, brown sugar, kosher salt and cayenne pepper. Cook on low heat until brown sugar and salt is dissolved. Let cool so that the marinade does not "cook" the steaks. Pour cooled marinade over steaks. Cover and place in the refrigerator and marinate, turning once, for 3 hours.

2. Preheat lightly greased grill to 450°F (high setting). Remove steaks from marinade, discarding marinade. Place steaks on a baking sheet and baste each steak with 1 teaspoon olive oil. Pour lime juice over steaks. In a small bowl, combine Krazy salt and ground ginger and sprinkle over steaks. Gently press into steaks.

3. Grill steaks for 2 minutes per side, with grill lid closed, or until internal temperature reaches 145°F.

You'll Need

- 6 (1-inch thick) tuna steaks
- 2 cups water
- 1/2 cup packed brown sugar
- 1 tablespoon kosher salt
- 1/2 teaspoon cayenne pepper
- 2 tablespoons olive oil, divided
- Juice of 2 limes
- 1 teaspoon Jane's Krazy Mixed-Up Salt
- 3/4 teaspoon ground ginger

Smoking Optional

Preheat smoker to 225°F. Remove tuna from marinade. Sprinkle with olive oil, lime juice and spice mix and place on middle rack of smoker. Smoke for 1 1/2 hours, testing for doneness after 1 hour, or until internal temperature reaches 145°F.

You'll Need

- 1 (15-ounce) bottle of soy sauce

- 5 cloves garlic, minced

- Juice of 1 large lemon

- 6 tablespoons rosemary-garlic seasoning, divided

- 1 rib end pork loin roast (about 4 pounds)

GRILLED PORK LOIN ROAST
Serves 6 to 8

When wrapping this pork loin roast, make a "boat" with heavy-duty aluminum foil. Stack three long sheets of aluminum foil together. Place the roast in the middle of the foil and gather both of the long ends at the top. Roll those ends down toward the roast together. Fold up the sides and seal tightly. By using this method, instead of rolling the roast in foil, you contain the juices and avoid spilling them when you unwrap the roast at the end of the grilling process. The juices are so flavorful, so I poured them over the sliced roast and served to my guests.

Instructions

1. In a small bowl, combine soy sauce, garlic, lemon juice and 2 tablespoons of rosemary-garlic seasoning to make marinade. Reserve 1/2 cup for basting. Place roast in a deep pan and cover with marinade. Sprinkle top of roast generously with 2 tablespoons of rosemary-garlic seasoning. Cover and refrigerate overnight, turning at least twice during marinating. After turning, sprinkle other side generously with remaining 2 tablespoons rosemary-garlic seasoning.

2. Preheat lightly greased grill to 350°F (medium setting).

3. Remove meat and place on grill. Cook directly over the hottest part of the coals for 1 minute on each side to brown. Move loin roast to one side of the fire, cook with indirect heat (see page 11) with grill lid closed for 1 hour, turning once after 30 minutes. Baste with reserved marinade when turning. Baste again and wrap in aluminum foil. Cook over indirect heat for an additional 1 1/2 hours or until internal temperature reaches 160°F. Keep your fire hot, but do not cook directly over it. Remove from grill and slice and serve with your favorite sides!

GRILLED MEXICAN BURGERS
Serves 4

My brother Don and I were in El Salto, Mexico, filming a cooking video for ESPN. We loved the authentic Mexican food during that trip and have found many ways to bring those flavors into our own dishes. The lime and cilantro in these burgers gives a kick of flavor and the Jalapeño-Lime mayo is so dadgum good I even dipped my French fries in it!

Instructions

1. Preheat lightly greased grill to 400°F (medium-high setting).

2. **Jalapeño-Lime Mayonnaise:** In small bowl, stir together mayonnaise, lime zest, lime juice and jalapeño.

3. In a medium bowl, gently mix together beef, cilantro, green onion, jalapeño, garlic, chili powder, lime zest and salt. Shape into 4 patties, each about 3/4 inch thick. Grill burgers, with grill lid closed, turning once, for 8 to 10 minutes or until internal temperature reaches 145°F. Top each burger with 1 slice cheese. Grill for 1 minute or until cheese is melted. Spread each roll with Jalapeño-Lime Mayonnaise. Place lettuce on rolls and top with burgers.

El Salto — a dadgum good trip!

You'll Need

Jalapeño-Lime Mayonnaise

- 1/2 cup mayonnaise
- 2 teaspoons grated lime zest
- 2 tablespoons fresh lime juice or to taste
- 1 tablespoon finely chopped jalapeño

- 1 1/2 pounds ground beef chuck (80% lean)
- 1/4 cup chopped cilantro
- 2 tablespoons thinly sliced green onion
- 1 jalapeño, finely chopped
- 2 teaspoons minced garlic
- 2 teaspoons chili powder
- 1 teaspoon grated lime zest
- 3/4 teaspoon salt
- 4 slices Monterey Jack cheese
- 4 Kaiser rolls or Mexican bolillo rolls, split
- 2 cups shredded iceberg lettuce

GRILLED SALSA
Makes 2 cups

It's important to remove the membrane and seeds from the tomatoes for this salsa. If you don't, the salsa will be too runny. You don't want to overprocess this salsa either — leave it chunky. We had a football party at our lake house and this salsa didn't stay around for long. Enjoy it with tortilla chips or serve it with the Flat Iron Steak Tacos and Alicia's Guacamole on page 201.

Instructions

1. Preheat lightly greased grill to 350°F (medium setting).

2. Slice tomatoes in half and remove membranes and seeds. Grill tomatoes, red onion, garlic and jalapeño, with grill lid closed, for 5 minutes or until softened and grill marks appear. Remove from grill and let cool.

3. Peel tomatoes and garlic. Remove seeds from jalapeño. In a food processor, combine tomatoes, red onion, garlic, jalapeño, cilantro, lime juice and salt. Pulse 3 times or until salsa is blended but still chunky. Serve immediately or cover and refrigerate until ready to serve. Serve with tortilla chips.

You'll Need

- 6 fresh Campari or Roma (plum) tomatoes (about 1 pound)
- 1/2 small red onion
- 2 cloves garlic
- 1 fresh jalapeño
- 3 tablespoons chopped fresh cilantro
- 3 tablespoons fresh lime juice
- 1/4 teaspoon kosher salt
- Tortilla chips

You'll Need

- 2 pounds fresh salmon, well chopped

- 1 tablespoon + 1 teaspoon "DADGUM That's Good!"™ Seasoning (page 12)

- 2 teaspoons lime pepper

- 1/4 teaspoon freshly ground black pepper

- Garlic salt (optional)

- 8 white or whole wheat hamburger buns, split and toasted

- Mayonnaise

- Fresh basil leaves

- Tomato slices

GRILLED SALMON BURGERS

Serves 8

It is crucial to follow the step of using heavy-duty foil in this recipe. The salmon patties are delicate and will fall through the grill grates or stick. Also, the foil allows the patties to cook in their own juices, which punches up the flavor significantly. Another option would be to make the patties and put them in the freezer for about an hour to let them set before grilling — do not completely freeze.

Instructions

1. Preheat lightly greased grill to 400°F (medium-high setting).

2. In a large bowl, combine salmon, seasoning, lime pepper and black pepper. Form mixture into 8 patties, each about 3/4 inch thick. Place patties on a sheet of heavy-duty aluminum foil.

3. Place foil with patties on grill, close to the coals, and grill, with grill lid closed, for 3 minutes on each side (do not place patties directly onto grill). Remove from grill. Sprinkle with garlic salt, if using. Serve on white or whole wheat buns with mayonnaise, fresh basil leaves and tomato.

The first time my wife's parents had me over for dinner, I left quite an impression. Tonya's father (Wes) grilled ribs for dinner and her mother (Shirley) made the side dishes. We were sitting around the table in the formal dining room and I started on my first rib. I lost my grip on the rib and it flung across the room and ricocheted off of the wall and onto the carpet! Two months later, my brother Don came over to Tonya's parent's house for dinner. Grilled ribs made a return appearance on the menu and — you're not gonna believe this — Don did the exact same thing! I'm surprised Wes and Shirley didn't make us dine in the backyard with the dogs from then on!

Top Left: *Tonya's family right before I came into their lives*
Top Right: *Wes loved cooking breakfast for us.*
Middle and Bottom: *Nothing like family time with Wes!*

GRILLED BABY BACK RIBS
Serves 4

Instructions

1. Preheat lightly greased grill to 400°F (medium-high setting).

2. In a medium bowl, combine garlic pepper, salt, onion powder and paprika.

3. Rub mixture on ribs and grill for 1 hour, turning every 10 minutes. Grill using indirect heat (see page 11) with grill lid closed.

4. **BBQ Sauce:** In a saucepan over low heat, combine ketchup, brown sugar, lemon juice and steak sauce and simmer for 10 minutes.

5. Remove ribs from grill and apply BBQ Sauce to ribs. Then place back on grill with meat side up for 10 minutes.

You'll Need

- 2 tablespoons garlic pepper
- 1 teaspoon salt
- 1 teaspoon onion powder
- 1 teaspoon paprika
- 2 slabs baby back ribs

BBQ Sauce

- 1/3 cup ketchup
- 1/2 cup packed brown sugar
- Juice of 1 large lemon
- 1/3 cup A1 Steak Sauce

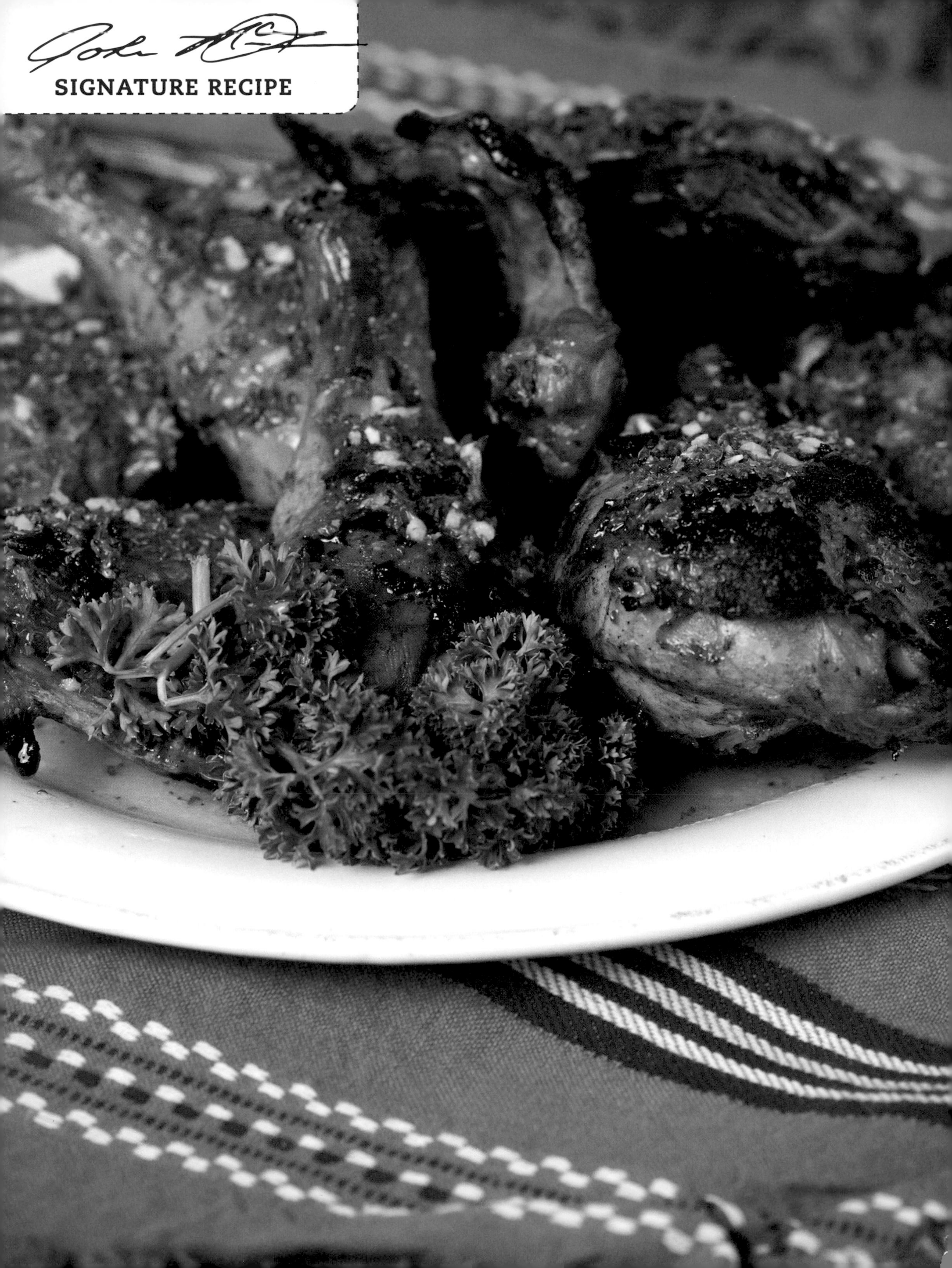
SIGNATURE RECIPE

BRINED CHICKEN WITH LEMON VINAIGRETTE

Serves 4

This chicken with lemon vinaigrette is so dadgum good, I would bet you won't have any leftovers. But, if you do, place the chicken in a shallow dish and drizzle with the vinaigrette and reheat. You can also cut up the chicken and serve over salad or pasta with the vinaigrette. There will be a significant difference in the grilling time for boneless versus bone-in chicken. Make sure you carefully monitor the internal temp. The chicken is done when it reaches 165°F.

Instructions

1. In an extra-large bowl, combine chicken, water, 1/4 cup of salt and sugar. Cover and refrigerate overnight. Remove chicken, rinse to remove excess salt and pat dry.

2. Lemon Vinaigrette: In a blender or food processor, combine lemon juice, parsley, garlic, remaining 1/4 teaspoon of salt and pepper and blend until smooth. With the machine running, gradually add oil through the feed tube. Set aside.

3. Preheat lightly greased grill to 400°F (medium-high setting).

4. Grill chicken, with grill lid closed, turning occasionally, for 25 to 35 minutes or until internal temperature reaches 165°F and chicken is no longer pink inside. Drizzle with lemon vinaigrette and serve immediately. Garnish with fresh parsley, if using.

You'll Need

- 3 pounds assorted chicken pieces

- 2 quarts water

- 1/4 cup + 1/4 teaspoon kosher salt, divided

- 2 tablespoons granulated sugar

Lemon Vinaigrette

- 1/4 cup fresh lemon juice

- 1/4 cup chopped fresh parsley

- 2 cloves garlic, peeled

- 1/4 teaspoon freshly ground black pepper

- 1/3 cup olive oil

- Fresh parsley sprigs (optional)

Bone-In Option
You can also use bone-in chicken, which gets more tender results, but grill for 15 to 20 minutes longer or until internal temperature reaches 165°F.

COCONUT-MARINATED CHICKEN KABOBS

Serves 4

When you're in a hurry, you can marinate this recipe for only 30 minutes before placing on the grill. If you've got more time to spare, it's always good to allow the ingredients more time to marinate. Don't forget to cut the chicken into 1-inch pieces before marinating so that all sides of each piece of chicken get coated. Double the crushed red pepper and jalapeño if you want more of a kick.

Instructions

1. In a medium bowl, whisk together coconut milk, 2 tablespoons of the lime juice, garlic, jalapeño, salt and red pepper flakes to taste. Place chicken in a resealable plastic bag. Add coconut mixture, coating chicken well. Seal bag and refrigerate, turning occasionally, for 30 minutes or for up to 4 hours.

2. Preheat lightly greased grill to 400°F (medium-high setting).

3. Soak wooden skewers in water for 30 minutes. Remove chicken from marinade, discarding marinade. Thread chicken onto skewers, alternating with pineapple, red and green bell peppers and onion.

4. Grill skewers, with grill lid closed, turning every 3 to 4 minutes, for 12 minutes or until chicken is no longer pink inside and vegetables are tender. Drizzle with remaining lime juice before serving.

You'll Need

- 4 (8-inch) wooden skewers, soaked in water for 30 minutes
- 3/4 cup light or regular coconut milk
- 4 tablespoons fresh lime juice, divided
- 2 garlic cloves, minced
- 1 teaspoon finely chopped fresh jalapeño (about 1 small)
- 1 teaspoon kosher salt
- 1/4 to 1/2 teaspoon crushed red pepper flakes
- 1 1/2 pounds boneless skinless chicken breasts, cut into 1-inch pieces
- 1 1/2 cups fresh pineapple chunks (1-inch pieces)
- 1 medium red bell pepper, cut into 1-inch pieces
- 1 medium green bell pepper, cut into 1-inch pieces
- 1 red onion, cut into 1-inch pieces

EASY GRILLED CAJUN WINGS
Serves 6 to 8

In the McLemore house, we entertain a lot. Our kids have friends over often and feeding a large crowd is an almost weekly event. Chicken wings are a sure crowd-pleaser and we've cooked them just about every way imaginable. These grilled wings have become more popular than fried wings in our home. In fact, they never make it to the table. The crowd lingers around the grill and eats them as I take them off! If you've got a brave crowd to feed, use extra-hot sauce instead of mild.

You'll Need

- 2 1/2 teaspoons Cajun seasoning
- 1 1/2 teaspoons paprika
- 1 1/2 teaspoons dried oregano
- 2 pounds chicken wings or drumettes
- 1/2 cup orange juice
- 1/4 cup mild hot sauce
- 1/4 cup fresh lemon juice
- 2 tablespoons Worcestershire sauce

Instructions

1. In a small bowl, combine Cajun seasoning, paprika and oregano.

2. Place wings in a large shallow dish or resealable plastic bag. Add Cajun spice mixture, tossing well. Add orange juice, hot sauce, lemon juice and Worcestershire sauce, mixing well. Cover or seal and refrigerate, turning occasionally, for 4 hours or for up to 8 hours. For more spicy flavor, leave wings in the marinade a little longer.

3. Preheat lightly greased grill to 350°F (medium setting).

4. Remove wings from marinade, discarding marinade. Grill wings, with grill lid closed, turning every 3 to 4 minutes, for 20 to 25 minutes or until internal temperature reaches 165°F. Serve immediately.

When we asked my daughter Brooke what she wanted for dinner at her 16th birthday party, she didn't hesitate to request her favorite meal — steak and lobster. The rest of the crowd dined on hot dogs and hamburgers while the birthday girl enjoyed her feast of grilled steak and lobster with butter. The herb butter from this recipe works well on steak or lobster. It doesn't have to be your 16th birthday for you to enjoy this meal!

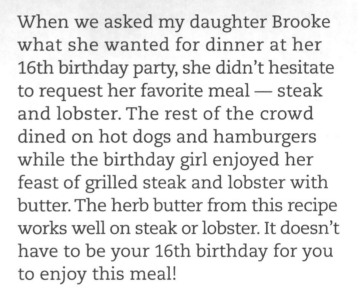

Top Left: *She thought steak and lobster was dadgum good.*
Top Right: *J-Mac and Brooke were always full of mischief.*
Middle: *Even as a baby she loved hangin' with me.*
Bottom Left: *She still loves hangin' with me.*
Above: *Great milestone day — high school graduation!*

You'll Need

- 4 (1/2-inch thick) rib-eye steaks (about 1 1/2 to 2 pounds)

- 1 teaspoon sea salt

- 1 teaspoon freshly ground black pepper

- 2 tablespoons melted butter

Herb Butter

- 4 tablespoons melted butter

- 2 tablespoons finely chopped shallots

- 1 tablespoon chopped parsley

- 1 tablespoon chopped fresh chives

BROOKE'S GRILLED STEAKS WITH HERB BUTTER
Serves 4

Instructions

1. Preheat lightly greased grill to 400°F (medium-high setting).

2. Season both sides of steaks with salt and pepper and brush equally with 2 tablespoons of butter.

3. **Herb Butter:** In a small saucepan over low heat, melt 4 tablespoons of butter. Add shallots, parsley and chives and heat though.

4. Grill steaks, with grill lid closed, for 2 to 4 minutes per side (adjust time for desired degree of doneness). See Doneness Chart to the right for temperatures. Drizzle Herb Butter evenly over steaks.

Doneness Chart

125°F Rare

135°F Medium-Rare

145°F Medium

155°F Medium-Well

165°F Well Done

GRILLED APPLES
Serves 2 to 4

Apples stand up well to the grilling process. If you have an apple corer, core these apples and slice them in rings. The rings will be easier to place and turn on the grill. Serve them up solo or on top of vanilla ice cream with some warm caramel sauce.

You'll Need

- 2 Gala apples
- 2 tablespoons fresh lemon juice
- 2 tablespoons granulated sugar
- 1 teaspoon ground cinnamon
- 4 tablespoons melted butter
- Vanilla ice cream (optional)

Instructions

1. Preheat lightly greased grill to 400°F (medium-high setting).

2. Peel apples, core and cut into quarters. Sprinkle with lemon juice to keep from turning brown. Grill for 8 minutes.

3. In a small bowl, combine sugar and cinnamon. Turn apples, baste with butter and sprinkle with cinnamon-sugar mixture. Grill, with grill lid closed, for 2 minutes, flip and baste with butter and sprinkle with cinnamon-sugar mixture. Use caution when basting with butter because it will flare up. Grill for an additional 2 minutes

4. Remove from grill if you like apples crunchy or cook for 2 additional minutes on each side if you like apples more tender.

5. Serve these grilled apples with some vanilla ice cream, if using.

GRILLED TURKEY BREAST
Serves 6 to 8

You'll Need

- 1/2 cup fresh lime or lemon juice
- 5 tablespoons "DADGUM That's Good!"™ Seasoning (page 12)
- 1 tablespoon Creole mustard
- 1 turkey breast (5 to 6 pounds)

When it comes to cooking turkeys, my family is known for thinking outside of the oven. We deep-fry and smoke turkeys quite often and don't even consider oven-roasting our turkeys anymore. Another creative way to prepare turkey is by using the grill. Butterflying or flattening the turkey breast is a key step in this recipe for even grilling. Because the turkey breast is a large piece of meat, using indirect heat allows it to cook completely through without drying out.

Instructions

1. In a small bowl, combine lime juice, seasoning and Creole mustard, mixing well.

2. When you purchase turkey breast, ask your butcher to butterfly it, or after thawing, make a cut on top of turkey along the bone. Place on a cutting board and, with your hand, pound hard on the top of the breast. This should crack the breastbone and flatten the turkey breast. Rub turkey breast well with seasoning mixture and place in a large resealable freezer bag. Refrigerate, turning occasionally, for 8 hours.

3. Preheat lightly greased grill to 400°F (medium-high setting).

4. Remove meat from bag, reserving seasoning and juices. Grill turkey for 30 minutes, turning once. Remove turkey and wrap securely in foil, along with remaining juices and seasoning. Place on indirect heat (see page 11) and grill, with grill lid closed, for 2 hours or until internal temperature reaches 165°F.

My buddy Donald and I met when our daughters played softball together. We would travel together for softball tournaments. When everyone got tired of concession food and pizza delivery, we decided to grill out. Donald was always famous for his secret Wallerin' Chicken recipe. He didn't trust anyone with the recipe — not even his family. Because I am his dadgum good friend, he decided to let me take a peek at the recipe — and I decided to share it with all of you! There are three versions of this recipe: Hot, Dadgum Hot and "I Dadgum Dare Ya!" I like and recommend the Dadgum Hot, but love serving up the "I Dadgum Dare Ya!" version to my buddies and watching them sweat!

Top: *Me and Donald with our daughters, Tarah and Brooke.*
Middle: *High school ball and an inside joke with Tarah and Brooke.*
Bottom: *Me and my buddy Donald.*

DONALD'S WALLERIN' CHICKEN
Serves 8

Instructions

1. Preheat lightly greased grill to 350°F (medium setting).

2. Wallering Sauce: In a large saucepan over medium heat, combine apple cider vinegar, hot sauce, salt, black pepper and red pepper flakes. Bring sauce to a simmer for about 10 minutes.

3. Grill chicken, with grill lid closed, turning occasionally, for 50 minutes. After 40 minutes of grilling, with tongs or a sharp knife, stab each piece of chicken and create an opening for Wallering Sauce to seep into chicken. Remove chicken from grill and place in Wallering Sauce for 10 minutes, turning twice. Remove from sauce and serve.

Optional HOTNESS

- 1/2 cup cayenne pepper
- 1/4 cup Grace Hot Pepper Sauce (really hot stuff)
- 1 tablespoon habanero powder (really HOT STUFF)

1. In a pot large enough to waller your chicken, combine cayenne, hot sauce and habanero powder. Add chicken and let waller in the sauce for 30 minutes to 1 hour. Continue with Step 3 above.

You'll Need

Wallering Sauce

- 1/2 gallon apple cider vinegar

- 1/2 cup of your favorite liquid hot sauce (hotter the better for me)

- 1/2 cup salt

- 1/2 cup freshly ground black pepper

- 1/2 cup crushed red pepper flakes

- 8 large boneless skinless chicken breasts

HONEY-GARLIC PORK TENDERLOIN
Serves 6

This recipe calls for grilling the tenderloins directly on the grill rack for 20 minutes, turning every 2 minutes. A more forgiving method you can try is wrapping them. Refer to the instructions on making a foil "boat" on our recipe for Grilled Pork Loin Roast on page 173. If I'm not in a hurry, I always like to use this wrapping method for a juicy result.

Instructions

1. In a medium bowl, whisk together garlic, soy sauce, hot sauce, honey, Worcestershire sauce and pepper.

2. Place tenderloins in a large resealable plastic bag. Pour in marinade and refrigerate, turning occasionally, for 1 hour or for up to 8 hours.

3. Preheat lightly greased grill to 400°F (medium-high setting).

4. Remove pork from marinade, discarding marinade, and grill, with grill lid closed, turning every 2 minutes, for 20 minutes. Cook for an additional 10 minutes, turning halfway through cooking or until thermometer registers 155°F at thickest point and tenderloin is slightly pink in center.

5. Place pork on a cutting board. Loosely cover with foil and let stand for 10 minutes. Cut into slices.

You'll Need

- 2 cloves garlic, minced
- 1/3 cup regular or low-sodium soy sauce
- 1 tablespoon hot sauce
- 1 tablespoon honey
- 2 teaspoons Worcestershire sauce
- 1/4 teaspoon freshly ground pepper
- 2 pork tenderloins, trimmed (about 2 1/2 pounds)

GRILLED ZUCCHINI WITH ROSEMARY AND FETA CHEESE

Serves 4

I was at a trade show in Germany, smoking some BBQ for retailers in the European market. As a complement to the BBQ, we grilled up some zucchini, squash and onions. They were such a hit with the crowd at the show that I tried them out at home. My wife would eat feta on just about anything, so she tossed some feta on these warm grilled veggies. I must admit, that was the perfect finishing touch.

You'll Need

- 2 medium zucchini (about 3/4 pound), unpeeled and cut lengthwise into 1/4-inch slices

- 1 medium yellow squash, unpeeled and cut into 1/2-inch slices

- 1 small yellow onion, cut into 1/2-inch thick rounds

- 1/2 teaspoon kosher salt

- 1/4 teaspoon freshly ground black pepper

- 2 tablespoons olive oil

- 2 tablespoons fresh lemon juice

- 2 tablespoons finely chopped fresh rosemary

- 1/4 cup crumbled feta cheese or goat cheese

Instructions

1. Preheat lightly greased grill to 350°F (medium setting).

2. In a large shallow dish, combine zucchini, squash and onion. Sprinkle with salt and pepper. Drizzle with olive oil and lemon juice. Grill vegetables, with grill lid closed, turning occasionally, for 6 to 8 minutes or until tender. Remove from grill and sprinkle with rosemary and feta cheese. Serve warm or at room temperature.

GRILLED BLACKBERRY COBBLER
Serves 6

You may have read the title to this recipe and thought, "huh?!" Friend, let me introduce you to the awesome benefits of indirect grilling. As long as you aren't grilling directly over your flame or coals, you can cook some recipes you would normally bake in the oven on your grill. Free up your kitchen and let the grill do the work on this Blackberry Cobbler. You'll be the talk of the neighborhood when you pull your cobbler off the grill!

You'll Need

- 3 cups fresh blackberries
- 1 1/4 cups granulated sugar
- 1 cup self-rising flour
- 1 cup half-and-half cream
- 1/2 cup melted butter
- Vanilla ice cream

Instructions

1.   Preheat lightly greased grill to 350°F (medium setting).

2.   Place blackberries in a deep, round 10-inch aluminum foil pan. In a medium bowl, stir together sugar and flour. Add cream and melted butter and stir well. Pour mixture over berries.

3.   Place foil pan over indirect heat and grill, with grill lid closed, for 1 hour. Remove from grill and enjoy with your favorite vanilla ice cream!

GRILLED BANANA SUNDAES
Serves 4

While grilling these bananas over medium heat, make sure you move them around to prevent them from sticking. I would suggest using a spatula instead of tongs, since they become soft as you grill them. Leave enough room on the grill surface to roll them over with the spatula. The grilling process helps the cinnamon, butter and vanilla caramelize onto the bananas, adding flavor that far surpasses a plain ol' banana sundae.

Instructions

1. Preheat lightly greased grill to 350°F (medium setting).

2. Cut bananas in half lengthwise. Cut each piece in half crosswise. Place in a large shallow dish.

3. In a small bowl, stir together butter, cinnamon and vanilla. Brush butter mixture on both sides of bananas.

4. Grill bananas for 2 minutes on each side or until heated through. Be sure to use a spatula to move the bananas around gently during the grilling process to prevent sticking. Scoop ice cream into 4 serving dishes. Top evenly with bananas and drizzle with your favorite ice cream topping. Sprinkle evenly with pecans and desired toppings.

You'll Need

- 4 large ripe firm bananas
- 4 tablespoons butter, melted
- 1/4 teaspoon ground cinnamon
- 1/4 teaspoon vanilla extract
- 1 pint vanilla ice cream
- 1/2 cup caramel or chocolate ice cream topping, warmed
- 1/2 cup chopped pecans, toasted
- Toppings (optional)
  Sprinkles
  Toasted coconut
  Maraschino cherries

You'll Need

- 5 tablespoons butter

- 1/2 cup packed light brown sugar

- 1 tablespoon rum extract

- 1 teaspoon vanilla extract

- 1/2 teaspoon ground cinnamon

- Toasted chopped pecans (optional)

- Coconut (optional)

- 2 cups cubed fresh pineapple

- 4 scoops vanilla ice cream

GRILLED PINEAPPLE FOSTER
Serves 4

Before grilling pineapple, make sure your grill racks are completely clean and sprayed with nonstick spray. If you have any leftover "bits" on your grill racks, the pineapple will pick them up. You can leave the rings whole and place over ice cream, or cut the pineapple into bite-size cubes.

Instructions

1. Preheat lightly greased grill to 350°F (medium setting).

2. In a large saucepan, melt butter over medium heat. Add brown sugar, rum extract, vanilla and cinnamon. Cook, stirring often, until sugar is dissolved. Set aside and keep warm over low heat.

3. Toast pecans, if using, in a hot dry skillet over medium heat, stirring occasionally, for 4 minutes or until browned. Or toast in a 375°F oven with coconut, stirring twice, for 5 minutes.

4. Grill pineapple, with grill lid closed, for 1 to 2 minutes per side or until grill marks appear. Scoop ice cream into 4 individual serving bowls. Top evenly with pineapple and drizzle with sauce. Top with pecans and/or coconut, if using.

TRIPLE-THREAT GRILLED CHICKEN

Serves 6 to 8

My custom trailer grill is quite a conversation piece. Wherever we go, people seem to gravitate toward the grill. I have to admit, I'm pretty dadgum proud of it. In fact, the grill is known as my "baby." And my baby has come in handy during Masterbuilt events, whether we are cooking for the employees or serving food to the homeless at our local mission. My friend Jimmy built my trailer grill and gave me this recipe for Triple-Threat Grilled Chicken. He's a barbecue champion and when you eat this chicken you'll understand why. We may need to call Jimmy "the stork," since he delivered my baby and a dadgum good recipe!

Instructions

1. In a small bowl, combine garlic salt, red pepper flakes, black pepper and onion powder. Set aside.

2. Triple-Threat Marinade: In a large bowl, combine Worcestershire, soy sauce and teriyaki marinade, reserving 1 1/2 cups of marinade for later. In a large bowl, place chicken thighs and pour 3 cups of Triple-Threat Marinade over chicken and marinate for 30 minutes. Remove chicken from marinade, discarding marinade, and season on both sides with dry seasoning.

3. Preheat lightly greased grill to 350°F (medium setting).

4. Place chicken, skin-side down, on grill using indirect heat (see page 11) and grill, with grill lid closed, for 40 minutes, checking every 15 minutes, being careful not to overcook. Turn chicken and grill for an additional 20 minutes with skin-side up. Throughout the grilling process, baste frequently with reserved Triple-Threat Marinade, using a spray bottle. Chicken is done when internal temperature reaches 165°F or until juices run clear.

You'll Need

- 1 tablespoon garlic salt
- 1 tablespoon crushed red pepper flakes
- 1 teaspoon freshly ground black pepper
- 1 teaspoon onion powder

Triple-Threat Marinade

- 1 1/2 cups Worcestershire sauce
- 1 1/2 cups soy sauce
- 1 1/2 cups teriyaki marinade

- 12 chicken thighs, skin-on

My "baby."

GRILLED TOMATOES
Serves 8

We mention the benefits of indirect grilling throughout this book. You can reference our grilling tips on page 11 for more detailed info on direct versus indirect grilling. This is definitely a recipe that requires the indirect method of grilling. Even though you are placing the tomatoes on foil, make sure you position them away from the heat source. This allows them to cook without scorching the skin.

You'll Need

- 2 large tomatoes
- 1/2 teaspoon olive oil
- Steak seasoning
- 1/2 cup freshly grated Parmesan cheese

Instructions

1. Cut tomatoes in half, then score the inside membrane with a knife several times. Drizzle tomatoes with olive oil. Sprinkle with steak seasoning and Parmesan.

2. Preheat lightly greased grill to 350°F (medium setting).

3. Place tomatoes on a sheet of heavy-duty aluminum foil. Place foil with tomatoes on grill and grill over indirect heat, with grill lid closed, for 25 to 45 minutes. Check halfway through grilling, so the Parmesan cheese does not burn.

JAMAICAN-SPICED FLANK STEAK

Serves 4

When it comes to grilled steak, I'm a bit of a traditionalist. The sweet seasonings in this Jamaican-Spiced Flank Steak have turned my taste buds on their heels! You'll love the way the brown sugar and cinnamon create a crust on the edges of the steak. Searing on high heat on the grill help this process along. Slice this steak and serve on rice with a side of sliced pineapple.

Instructions

1. Marinade: In a medium bowl, combine orange juice, lime juice, ginger, brown sugar, salt, pepper and cinnamon. Place steak in a large resealable plastic bag and pour marinade over steak. Seal and refrigerate, turning occasionally, for 2 to 8 hours.

2. Preheat lightly greased grill to 400°F (medium-high setting).

3. Remove steak from marinade, discarding marinade. Grill steak, with grill lid closed, for 8 to 10 minutes per side or to desired doneness (5 to 6 minutes per side for rare, 6 to 7 minutes per side for medium-rare, 7 to 8 minutes per side for medium, 8 to 10 minutes per side for well-done). Remove from grill. Let stand for 10 minutes. Cut diagonally against the grain into thin slices and serve.

You'll Need

Marinade

- 1/3 cup fresh orange juice
- 2 tablespoons fresh lime juice
- 2 teaspoons freshly grated peeled ginger root
- 1/4 cup packed dark brown sugar
- 1 teaspoon kosher salt
- 1 teaspoon freshly ground black pepper
- 1/2 teaspoon ground cinnamon

- 1 flank steak (about 2 pounds)

Top Left: *Alicia tries to keep me smiling!*

Top Right: *Best friends forever!*

Middle: *Thumbs up for Alicia's first trip to QVC.*

Bottom: *Me and Tonya with Alicia and her husband, Gary.*

ALICIA'S GUACAMOLE
Serves 2 to 4

I have been blessed with a fantastic career in a family business called Masterbuilt. I have always said that our greatest asset is our people. The employees of Masterbuilt have contributed to my success and the ability to do what I love to do. This recipe was given to me by Alicia, who is not only a dear friend and fantastic employee but also a best friend to my wife and kids. She has been very instrumental in the success of my first cookbook and even more so with this one. She has been my writing buddy and one of the chief recipe testers. I had never been a fan of guacamole until I tried Alicia's at Masterbuilt one day. You'll love it on these Flat Iron Steak Tacos and you can also pair it with the Grilled Mexican Burgers on page 175. Alicia is the younger sister I never had and I'm so glad to have her as a part of our family!

Instructions

1. Cut each avocado lengthwise and remove seeds. Spoon out avocado flesh and place in a bowl. Squeeze half of the lime juice over avocado and chop with a spoon so mixture remains chunky. Slice Roma tomatoes lengthwise. Remove and discard seeds and membranes. Chop tomatoes. Add chopped tomatoes, red onion and fresh cilantro to avocado and stir gently to mix. Pour remaining lime juice over the mixture. Add garlic powder and kosher salt sparingly to taste.

You'll Need

- 2 ripe avocados
- Juice of 2 limes, divided
- 2 Roma (plum) tomatoes
- 2 tablespoons chopped red onion
- 2 tablespoons fresh chopped cilantro
- 1/8 teaspoon garlic powder or to taste
- 1/8 teaspoon kosher salt or to taste

FLAT IRON STEAK TACOS
Serves 4

Instructions

1. In a small bowl, combine chili powder, cumin and cayenne. Drizzle steak with lime juice. Rub spice mixture into steak and place in a large resealable plastic bag. Seal and refrigerate, turning occasionally, for at least 2 hours or for up to 8 hours.

2. Preheat lightly greased grill to 400°F (medium-high setting).

3. Grill steak, with grill lid closed, for 5 minutes on each side or until desired degree of doneness (5 to 6 minutes per side for medium, 6 to 7 minutes per side for medium-well, 7 to 8 minutes per side for well-done). Remove steak from grill. Let stand for 5 minutes, resting in juices. Cut steak diagonally across the grain into thin slices. Serve in tortillas with lettuce, tomatoes, cheese and desired toppings.

You'll Need

- 1 teaspoon chili powder
- 1 teaspoon ground cumin
- 1/8 teaspoon cayenne pepper
- 1 1/4 pounds flat iron steak
- 1/2 cup fresh lime juice
- 4 (8-inch) flour tortillas, warmed
- 1 cup shredded lettuce
- 2 medium tomatoes, chopped (about 1 cup)
- 1/4 cup shredded Cheddar cheese
- Salsa and/or sour cream (optional)

Acknowledgments

I never cease to feel humbled and blessed by the amazing people God has placed in my life. It's God that I thank for each one of those people and for His mercy and unending grace. "All things are possible" because of this grace. He is the real President/CEO of my company, Masterbuilt, and the leader of my life.

I want to thank my wife, Tonya, who does such a fine job raising our kids — and me! She supports everything I do — from leading a business, to writing a cookbook, to any other crazy adventure I take us on. Tonya is our family cheerleader and she's been capturing our memories for over 24 years. She was instrumental in gathering the photos and stories together for this book. Without her, I wouldn't be the man I am today.

My kids — Brooke, J-Mac and Bailey — inspire me. They are growing into responsible young adults and live true to their Christian faith. I'm better for having them in my life.

My parents — Dawson and Evelyn McLemore — are my absolute rock and foundation. This book is dedicated to my momma, who we lost on December 29, 2011. She was my angel. My dad (The Ole' Man) continues to be my hero and I never cease to be amazed by his work ethic. Thanks, Ole' Man, for setting the bar high.

My brother Don has been my business partner for nearly 40 years and my best friend for our whole lives. Thanks to Don and his wife, Lynne, for helping create so many of these memories.

Lisa Johnson, my assistant, for her dedication and loyalty at Masterbuilt, her friendship and her support with this cookbook.

Alicia McGlamory for taking photos, testing recipes, and helping write the stories that come to life on these pages, but most of all for her friendship with my family.

To all the folks at Team Masterbuilt — thanks for being a huge part of our success story. Thanks for being willing to share your dadgum good recipes for this book. I also want to thank the great team at InPrint for their friendship and their dedication on this project.

To all of the people we met along the way who contributed their recipes — I'm honored to be your fan and your friend.

Lastly, I want to thank YOU, for becoming a part of our DTG community. I hope you enjoy getting to know my family and friends as you read through our memories, and I hope you share these dadgum good recipes with your own family and friends.